GAVASKAR
Portrait of a Hero

Major Works by the Author:

The Growing With Language Series

Insights

Sunshine And Shadow

English For Special Purposes

GAVASKAR
Portrait of a Hero

Clifford Narinesingh

with

ESSAYS ON GAVASKAR
(Appended)

FOREWORD BY SIR GARFIELD SOBERS

ROYARDS PUBLISHING COMPANY

ROYARDS PUBLISHING COMPANY
UNION VILLAGE, CLAXTON BAY
TRINIDAD, WEST INDIES.
TEL: 809-659-2260
FAX: 809-659-3535

ISBN - 976 - 8052 - 69 - 4

First Published November 1995

Published by Royards Publishing Company.

Typeset by Soraya Gonsalves.
Printed by L. Rex. Printing Company, China

For
Dafod and Dwight

Acknowledgements

The author wishes to acknowledge books and periodicals and other reference material consulted (as listed in the bibliography or sources of reference) with special reference to the writings of Sunil Gavaskar, *The Record-breaking Gavaskar* by C.D. Clark, *A History of Indian Cricket* by Mihir Bose, extracts from Simon Wilde and Brunell Jones and other sources quoted during the course of the work.

Sir Garfield Sobers' Foreword and the contributions of Peter Roebuck, Mike Coward and Michael Gibbes have certainly made the work more expansive and enhancing.

Special recognition must be given to Leander Dias, Debasish Datta, Hemant Waingankar, Manohar Gavaskar, Marshneil (Pammi) Gavaskar, Rudy Lee Kong, Lall Maharaj, Ravi Chaturvedi, Kailash Anand, Anand Maharaj, Anil Ramdin, Stanley Jones, Balan Sundaram, V.S. Patil, Madhav Mantri, Milind Rege, Lokendra Partap Sahi (Sports Editor, Calcutta Telegraph) and Raj Singh Dungarpur for their support.

West Indian sports critic, Michael Gibbes has been particularly supportive through his critical comments and rewarding discussions.

Every effort has been made by the publishers to contact all the copyright owners but in some cases this has been impossible. Any such omissions will be rectified at the first opportunity.

Black and White Photographs:
  Patrick Eagar - *photos 1-5*
  Suman Chattopadhyay (Aajkaal) - *photos 7-8*
Back Cover Colour Photograph:
  Patrick Eagar

Contents

Foreword

Indian cricket has, over the years, produced some fine players, including in my lifetime the world-rated Vinoo Mankad, Subash Gupte and others, but none better than the subject of this book.

It was as captain of the West Indies in 1971 that I first had the pleasure of seeing the very young Sunil Gavaskar in his debut series. In his first Test (the second of the series), he hit 65 and 67 not out as India secured the only win and captured the rubber.

The other four matches were drawn, but young Gavaskar went on to amass 774 runs with four centuries - two in the final match at Trinidad - and a series average exceeding 150.

This was a phenomenal start to a Test career which was to continue to set new standards in courage and application, for India had no demon bowlers, yet Gavaskar continued whenever he played, to rewrite the record books, even though he was raised on spin.

There was one period when perhaps the cares of captaincy and other matters weighed him down and the customary avalanche was reduced to 50's. His teammate Dilip Doshi, invited me, as I was then living in Australia, to have a look and offer a couple of tips.

I immediately noticed that Sunil was not getting behind the line. He was too often square-on outside off-stump and therefore would offer too many chances to slip and gully. It is to his great credit that one little word in his ear was enough and he was soon again coping with Thomson, Lillee, Alderman, Lawson and all the rest that Australia had to throw at him.

After I retired, Sunil again toured West Indies in 1976 under the captaincy of Bedi. He showed his true colours and in Trinidad when West Indies gave India 400 to win, Sunil was the main factor in leading his team to win, a feat that was only previously done by Australia against England.

Sunil will always stand out in my memory as one of the greatest batsmen of all time. He played against the toughest teams with some of the greatest fast bowlers and he stood the test of time for two decades, truly emphasizing the class of this great player.

This book will be a lesson for all young players and a collector's item for all who study the great enduring performances in the game of cricket.

I wish him all the best for this new book and I hope it will be very successful.

Sir Garfield Sobers

Author's Preface

To preserve an admirable past is to give relevance, meaning and recognition to its historical significance as an insignia of a civilization and a memoir for future generations.

This biographical work on Sunil Gavaskar is a gesture of recognition of one who has contributed to the game by virtue of his craft as a batsman and his significance on and off the playing field. Though it encompasses his life and career, it makes no ambitious claim as the definitive biographical record but attempts to focus on the personality, the process of his flight to heroism, his presence as a cricketer and his impact on the game.

Sunil Gavaskar rose to eminence from his early youth to mature retirement and was acclaimed a cricketing hero, distinguished and exalted. His craft in its form, technique, skill and variety is a symbol of the indestructibility of the pleasures of the game of cricket. He shaped a career which has impacted on and changed the psyche of Indian cricket and inspired his fellow countrymen. In the process he acted as a catalyst for future players and the progress of cricket in India. This is now clearly seen in the new batting talent emerging in India and the greater respect Indian cricket now earns on the international scene. A new spirit of optimism now informs India's cricketing presence.

The work attempts to re-acquaint cricket lovers and supporters of Gavaskar who were delighted and fascinated by his prowess. It celebrates his achievements, looks critically at a career with its brilliant flashes and its less luminous periods. It is hoped that the chequered career which emerges will reflect relevance and significance. While statistical records are useful in assessing achievement and contribution one's sensitivity must focus on character in situation. In this context dissection of averages and analysis of scores are not the emphases. The objective is to relate to sensibilities that recognize the larger implications of his presence as a national hero and as a person whose flight to heroism was fraught with predicaments, dilemmas and controversies.

During the past few decades we have read of or seen batsmen with varied approaches to the game. Some of them are characterized by or known for special techniques and approaches. There is the crowd pleaser or entertainer in his cavalier style, aggressive in intent and execution; there is the dogged, monotonous batsman bent on accumulating scores and records without the 'larger' interests of the game, perhaps one of the evils of professionalism, and then there are those who delight gracefully blending skill, technique, correctness and aggression.

Sunil Gavaskar was not the loose cavalier, neither the dogged routine opener. Though he accumulated high scores it never seemed as if he harboured an inordinate passion for records but his was an approach that betrayed a deep impulse to perform with distinction for his self-esteem, his team and his country's pride.

The writing is done with a commitment to undisputed facts, free of sensational and fanciful anecdotes which at times embellish the recorded careers of past personalities. It attempts to be free of reckless indictment or dogmatic interpretation of the game. It tries to recall faithfully the pursuits of one excelling in achievement and also faltering at times as heroes do.

It is hoped that this work as well as others in the same genre will add to the rich body of literature in the realm of cricket. In expressing the spirit of the game and of the age, an attempt is made to be faithful to the craft of writing in the same manner in which Gavaskar the batsman has been faithful to his craft.

Clifford Narinesingh

CHAPTER 1

Unheralded Dramatic Entry

Yet how he flashed unto the scene, how like a romantic hero with a sword that could know no tarnish, no graceless flow.

Edmund Blunden: Cricket Country

With great fervour and fascination, the people of the Caribbean Isles or 'Sunny Isles', a place of tropical beauty and leisured life, pursue and engage passionately in sports, particularly the game of cricket; theirs is an intensity of feeling and passion comparable with other cricketing countries. Nothing impedes spontaneous enjoyment of exciting cricket, the abounding love for entertainment, one of the strongest passions of the human mind; nothing detracts from spectators' absorption and thrill. It is with a sense of pride that they ponder on the game and discuss its glamour, its pleasures and its uncertainties.

Cricket serves as an anodyne for the many who are starved of entertainment. When played at its highest level, there is a temporary relief from the rigours of routine existence; to many it serves as a refuge and an escape from arduous living.

As for the cricketers, the West Indians have always enjoyed a reputation for cricketing talent and unique ability; from its simple beginnings West Indian cricket rose to superiority over the traditionally formidable cricketing countries such as Australia and England and this has created an aura which inspires awe and admiration. Over the past four decades the islands have produced a blend of cricket that excites, exhilarates and refreshes, a body of rich talent, a uniqueness of style; a cricket not conforming too rigidly to the theoretic schemes and designs of the game or orthodox approaches, but a style

1

and form original and innovative in batting, devastating and penetrative in its versatile pace bowling.

A touring team to the West Indies is always welcomed or greeted with pleasant anticipation. For months prior to the contest, among the cricketing multitude there is the village critic, the casual supporter, the uninitiated as well as the more sophisticated, objective and professional analyst either perched on office desks, bar stools, on pavements, playing fields or sandy beaches, giving expression to thoughts and feelings on the game.

It was the year 1971 when we in the West Indies were expecting the arrival of the Indians; it was during the early part of the year, which we loosely term the dry season or an early summer, for here there is no great divide, no special demarcation of the seasons. It was a period teeming with the spirit of expectation and desire for delightful cricket but it was also a time not without its agony, dissension, rage, anger, frustration and hurt. The evils of island rivalry surfaced and manifested itself, each island staking claim for its local heroes. This was further aggravated by conflict over the choice of umpires. Such controversies and aggressive lobbying for island dominance and supremacy almost marred the proceedings during 1971. However, the prejudices and bickering were eventually put to rest in the interest of the game and we were prepared to welcome the Indians on their third visit to the Caribbean.

Everyone involved in the game, either at player or spectator level, was eager for good refreshing cricket but it was generally accepted that India did not possess the combination of batting skills and bowling ability to seriously challenge our reputed prowess in all aspects of the game. In the area of pace bowling the Indians, with the exception of the period (before World War II) in which Mohammed Nissar and Amar Singh played, never seemed to concentrate or show deep interest in the skill of fast bowling, so urgently necessary if one is to engage in serious competitive cricket. Their emphasis on spin and reliance on their batting talent did not give them the balance needed.

In the previous tour to the West Indies the Indians were demoralized completely through a 5-0 West Indian victory.

But in retrospect, the series between India and the West Indies in 1971 was charged with a special grandeur, a graceful season of cricket, that in a sense, transcended the routine contest of victor and vanquished. It was full of achievement, absorbing and delightful cricket, competitive and combative. On both sides there were outstanding displays - Dilip Sardesai, Eknath Solkar, Bedi and Venkataraghavan and the new hero, Sunil Gavaskar. The West Indian talent expressed itself notably in Gary Sobers, Rohan Kanhai and Charlie Davis; and on one occasion Jack Noreiga who had a startling performance capturing 9 wickets for 95 runs. India's cricket now appeared in its ascendancy. Its combative strength weakened the fabric of a formidable West Indian team, which included the vintage Sobers, Kanhai, Lloyd, and Gibbs. And there was the discovery, the emergence of a new batting phenomenon, one who on his demonstration of consistency, possessed prodigious talent and unfaltering powers of concentration.

Gavaskar, at the age of 21, made his entry into Test cricket, not as a sensational prodigy but as a cricketer of promise. Vijay Merchant in his advice to Indian cricketers before their Caribbean journey singled out Gavaskar: "Though he is the youngest player in the team, the senior players would do well to follow his example."

Before his Caribbean odyssey, his first class experience was limited to a few matches which yielded 811 runs. His highest score was 176 and his average 45. But he demonstrated a willing appetite for enormous totals; in an innings for Bombay University he acquired the unique score of 327. Wadekar, his captain at the time, with a keenness of observation and interest, expressed his confidence in him and inspired him to perform with pride.

The tour of 1971 saw him emerging as the "Little Master". Injury during the early part of the tour prevented his playing in the early matches and the first Test at Sabina, Jamaica, but his first first-class match yielded a promising 82, only to be followed by increasingly favourable innings of 125 and 63 at Guaracara Park in South Trinidad.

A sterling performance in his first class debut, in which he, perhaps through providential grace, scored the quite amazing victory run at Queen's Park Oval, Trinidad, was an expression of the role he assumed in being a major contributor to India's gallant victory in the series. It was a graceful entry into the highest level of cricket. During the series, after his initial success in scoring 65 and 67 not out in his first Test, he further announced his presence with 116 and 64 not out at Bourda, Guyana. It was his first Test century, only to be followed by a tiny blemish in scoring only one run in the first innings of the fourth Test at Kensington Oval, Barbados. But this was quickly rectified in the second innings with a resounding 117 not out. The fifth and final Test on his revisit to Queen's Park Oval was the crowning achievement. Here centuries in both innings -124 and 220 - brought his aggregate to 774 runs with an average of 154.80, a phenomenal and fascinating display of batting prowess.

The central theme of the tour turned out to be the battle for supremacy and dominance between Gavaskar's craft and the armoured arsenal of pace- the 'glamorized' willow and the lethal missile wielded at it with varying degrees of pace and intensity. The drama unfolded as the tour progressed. The batsman, small in stature, heroic in deed, weakening a moderately fiery pace attack with remarkable skill, courage and daring display of batsmanship. In the process Uton Dowe's, the young Jamaican pace bowler, reputation suffered, his strength of pace virtually reduced to dull mediocrity, and the West Indian team, universally acknowledged for its stature, demoralized and humbled.

Gavaskar, positive and gracefully aggressive, provided excitement and thrill for an audience, which, whatever its prejudices and loyalty, loves to witness daring encounters;

here the onslaught of willow on leather or the cartwheeling of stumps on the field. As an opening batsman his approach to his role and his initial encouraging success against experienced opponents with a reputation for vintage cricket talent in both departments of batting and bowling made him all the more confident and zealous, made him demonstrate his skill with ease and comfort throughout the series.

Here was a fledgling, promising in talent in the country of his birth, introduced to new landscape, new setting, new conditions, new faces. He had left the repose of his castle, his sanctum sanctorum where the mind is free and undisturbed, like a young pioneer seeking new frontiers but entering into new perplexities. Many Test cricketers have disclosed their feelings of awe and apprehension on such tours. Gavaskar was no exception to this for he was conscious of a new environment, public opinion and public gaze. Embedded in him was the desire to perform for his self-esteem, team and country, particularly against a team unique in its flair, flamboyance, fiery bowling, technique, method and style. Any new player has to critically study the West Indian approach if he is to meet the challenge with success. He was beset with apprehension, not with the prints of Friday's foot, but the footprints of pace.

Against this background and the knowledge of the hazards of the game, Gavaskar's mission or primary thrust was to carve an image, not realizing later on in his career, it would be consumed into an artifice of eternity. His success assumed a larger dimension of greatness for here was an inexperienced batsman who had journeyed on this expedition coming from a country virtually lacking in genuine pace, and in response demonstrating his ability to negotiate it with consummate ease.

Gavaskar's innings at Guaracara Park against Trinidad together with his Test debut scores of 65 and 67 not out were not merely the mixture of labour and learning with enthusiasm, but enthusiasm fused with freedom, authority, rhythm and vitality. He contributed handsomely to a seven wicket victory over the West Indies. Wisden records that Gavaskar completed a memorable debut by hitting the winning boundary. It was truly a dramatic and memorable entry to the game at its highest level.

Victory, however ecstatic and joyful, never overwhelmed him to the point where he became complacent. In his early autobiography, "Sunny Days" Gavaskar recalls: "But we were well aware that the West Indies were smarting under defeat, and we were determined to see that one success did not make us complacent," and in an expression of personal national pride asserts "It has always been a matter of great pride that I was able in my very first Test, to be associated with India's maiden Test victory against the West Indies and that too in the lion's den."

With the first victory recorded in the second Test, his debut Test, at the Queen's Park Oval, Port of Spain, the Indians full of courage and energy, journeyed to Guyana to explore the rich possibilities of gaining ascendancy in the series and securing a prominent place in the history of cricket and in the literature of the times.

In the third Test in Guyana, the West Indies in an enterprising and positive manner were off to a good opening start and eventually amassed a total of 363 in the first innings. Though a relatively good score with which to challenge an opposing team, it was never a heroic one. Again Gavaskar's might and consistency, fast becoming powerful and recognizable, overpowered the pace bowling. Together with Ashok Mankad he gave India a sound opening partnership of 72 and then, with Vishwanath, an exciting stand of 116. India seemed to relish the conditions at Bourda. His century, the first of the series and his debut Test century, came with a glorious and aggressive cover drive for four; it assumed the stamp of authority and pride. His score of 116 was an indication of his blossoming craft and this was evident when he followed up with 64 not out in the second innings.

Ted Dexter in observing Gavaskar's career as it matured, noted that "if there was a single part of his batting style which accounts for consistent success against the strongest attacks in the world, it is the straightness of his bat." Dexter continues "his ability to show the full face of the blade hanging down in a perfect perpendicular, wins him acclaim from among connoisseurs of batting as having the broadest bat in the game, next to Peter May." We in the West Indies were very fortunate to see this broad bat which Dexter lauds.

Gavaskar's prolific form alarmed both the West Indian contingent of players and spectators. His consistency was reassuring for his team and his performance at Bourda ensured that the West Indian total of 363 was not unattainable; in fact India managed to outscore the West Indies total by a very slender margin of 13 runs.

The match progressed, but no one expected a decisive outcome. Sobers and Davis were impressive in the West Indian reply, for both scored centuries. Eventually with a target of 294 to be made in 90 minutes, India responded bravely with Gavaskar and Mankad exploiting the favourable conditions of play. There was no tension, no impending disaster; the atmosphere was ripe for free and exuberant batting. Here again Gavaskar was undefeated with another half century to his credit. This continuing stream of success was amazing and made one wonder what limits there were to it.

Gavaskar in his "Sunny Days" comments:
"My personal Test aggregate had gone up to 312 in four innings, twice not out and an average of 156." He continues, "I was in good form," an indication that he was achieving mastery over the prevailing conditions, in particular the bowling; he was settling in with confidence. As a caring team person he was pleased with Mankad's and Vishwanath's form, but concerned with Dilip Sardesai's pulled muscle for he looked to his full team's performance if they were to sustain their triumphal march. As for his own image on achieving the first

of his many landmarks to follow he recalls, "many people must be wondering as to what is the feeling when one gets a century in Tests. My own reaction was simply to think of my parents who had given me every encouragement and who would be beaming when the news reached them." Here is an assertion of one's close bonding and familial ties, inculcated and developed from childhood. It testifies to the shaping of a character, enriched with gratitude and humanity.

The young Gavaskar was preoccupied seriously with the prospect of encountering the reputed express paceman Wesley Hall in Barbados in India's match prior to the fourth Test. He recalls his apprehension when facing a bowler for the first time, particularly a bowler of Hall's reputation. Having failed in the first innings through a run-out decision, his determination to make amends was urgent. His quest to conquer and gain mastery is expressed here when he speaks of his second innings: "In Hall's second over, when he bounced at me, I played the best hook shot I ever played. The ball went skimming to the mid-wicket boundary." It is this sense of mastery and the pride of success that made him realize his burning ambition to achieve with distinction. He had never thought of himself in this master role before his experience in the Caribbean, but honestly hoped to simply perform creditably for his and his country's glory.

The child who flourished within the compound walls and on the uneven bouncy wickets of the playground, through his efforts and determination, now came to the fore with the same desire and dedication to the game. And it was this quality of performance, particularly against fast bowlers, that Gavaskar cherished; it inspired him to the formidable force he eventually became.

With a great measure of confidence built on the strong aggregate that he enjoyed, Gavaskar entered the fourth Test at Bridgetown. Here performances from Lewis, Kanhai, Davis and Sobers contributed to an enviable and enormous score of 501 for 5 wickets declared, a not surprising feat for the West Indies on this ground. The strength and quality of India's batting were tested in the face of an imposing total and the often dreadful task of batting for the last forty minutes of the day's play, in this case, the second day's play.

The promising fast bowler, sometimes described as a fast medium pacer, Uton Dowe of Jamaica, was selected for this game. Dowe, young and energetic, was capable of producing some fast, dangerous spells. Gavaskar described him as fast but not as fast as he was reckoned to be. To an encouraging capacity crowd, Dowe engaged in a battle against the opening pair, Gavaskar and Mankad, in quickly fading light. In his opening spell, he had Gavaskar undecided, attempting to hook a ball rising from a good length. This was the end of his innings and the first failure of the series - a score of one run and a disappointing exit. The West Indian critics and crowd in their optimism, a spirit greatly needed at this time, felt Dowe's pace was the decisive response to Gavaskar's obdurate resistance.

With Gavaskar's early dismissal, Sardesai, consistent on this tour, and ably partnered by Solkar, again came to India's rescue contributing greatly to the score of 347, and thus ensuring that the Indians saved the follow-on. Sardesai's contribution to India's success in the Caribbean was invaluable. This rescue mission was reminiscent of the first Test at Kingston when Sardesai plucked courage and summoned his form and skill to steer India to relative safety. Here in this match out of India's 347 total, the last four wickets amassed 277 runs in defiance of the West Indian challenge.

In their second innings, with a lead of 194, the West Indian strategy was predictable and obvious - to accelerate the flow of runs and build a total respectable enough to gain a winning chance. India were set a score of 335 in 312 minutes if they were going to negotiate victory but captain Wadekar thought it was better or it was in the team's interest to enter into the final Test leading 1-0 than to put themselves at the risk of losing, in pursuit. India needed the staying power of a good early partnership to steer them to safety and this is what the captain relied on.

And Gavaskar responded bravely to his captain's call. Undaunted by his early first innings dismissal, he went on to secure India's safety and continuing 1-0 lead before travelling to the Queen's Park Oval for the final encounter. He played an innings which revealed his stature and progressive maturity in his punishment of Inshan Ali's loose wayward deliveries; and in responding to Dowe's and Holder's pace, rendered them quite ineffective in this second innings.

At 35 for 1, when Mankad departed, Gavaskar partnered his team-mates in a dedicated innings. Brunell Jones, sports writer and critic, recaptures the last few hours:

"1 for 35. But the minutes were clicking away into half-hours and hours. Sobers set a shining example to his men. He improvised, experimented, employed hunches and inspired his men. But Wadekar and Gavaskar were unbeaten at lunch. 1 for 69. Sobers struck immediately after the lunch resumption. Lloyd took a reflex catch when Wadekar mis-read the line of one of Sobers' deliveries and India had lost 2 for 71. Which became 3 for 79 as Sobers sent Vishwanath on his way back to the pavilion, caught by Shepherd for a duck. Gavaskar, unmoved by the goings-on, continued to play his strokes and by tea India had gone to 137 for 4. Jaisimha had been hit on the pad and had been given out LBW against Dowe.

Thereafter, the story of the day's play was written by Gavaskar, as he played beautifully for a series-preserving unbeaten 117. His century contained ten fours and the knock followed 116 and 74 not out at Georgetown and 65 and 67 not out at Port of Spain to absolve him of his first innings failure in this match.

Among the important side-issues to come out of the day's play was Gavaskar's dedicated approach. He faced 311 deliveries off which he scored 70 times. West Indies, on the other hand, got through the greatest number of overs (104) in any day's play of the entire game and in their frantic bid for victory, ten of the West Indians shared the attack, Sobers, 23-8-31-2, doing most of the work."

In his "Sunny Days" Gavaskar recalls:
"In the process I got a century (117 not out). It was purely a defensive innings since winning was out of the question. Yet I played my shots with confidence and authority, and a hook for 6 off a Dowe bouncer stands out in my memory."

The mastery of the challenge, the optimism exuded in describing his confidence and authority at the wicket, helped to fortify his already seemingly impregnable stature. Here he was, now epitomizing and distilling a mastery; the mastery of a bird in flight, soaring to new frontiers. It was a different flight, not of the mind or in the fancy, which took a confident India to the Queen's Park Oval and a Gavaskar in an apparently uninhibited quest for greater successes. For him it was becoming a summer luxury, especially when he began to enter the history books during the fifth Test. This he defined as his finest hour.

The final Test at the Oval contained the main elements of an interesting drama. This dramatic experience, real human experience, was enacted, and the players were real, not representative of characters on stage. It came to consciousness through its embodiment of human emotions with its accompanying tensions, suspense, frustrations, pleasures, feats of heroism. Long after the departure of the players, this sterling act remained happy in the memory of Gavaskar and the Indian contingent and in fact all who witnessed it.

It was a six day Test and this extended play period provided an opportunity for a decisive conclusion, save for interruption by rain. There was expectation and hope in the West Indian side, a team now with their last chance to salvage pride and honour through triumph; to restore their image as powerful and formidable. For the Indian team it was a test of endurance and will to continue in their achievement and to stake a claim as an established cricketing team for they had been expressing dominance and asserting confidence and strength as the series progressed. India entered the last Test at least with the knowledge that if even defeated they would not have been disgraced.

Sobers' reputation was challenged. His task to inspire his colleagues or team-mates to victory for the preservation of his own image, was urgent and compelling. During the series attention was focused on his captaincy and criticism was levelled at his leadership. Wadekar, his counterpart, showing shrewdness and tactical skill at the helm, urgently needed to win glory and demonstrate India's pride with a victory in the series.

An important element in the drama now unfolding was the West Indian crowd, which was experiencing the pangs of frustration, unease and an urgent desire to see its heroes dictating the proceedings of the game. They loved the game, the interest generated through the Indians fighting spirit, the brilliance of Gavaskar's batting; but they also yearned for a West Indian victory. To see one's heroes in the throes of defeat occasions emotional pain and hurt. In some countries, this hurt expresses itself in violence and aggression; but here in the West Indies this is seldom seen.

There is also a more complex issue which needs addressing, even briefly, but without oversimplification. It is the question of identity and national loyalty. Over the years it has become the norm to expect deviance from our local crowd's support for its team and I refer to those countries, Trinidad and Guyana, where Indians predominate. There is a significant ethnic body which lends support to India and Pakistan on their Caribbean tours; it is openly asserted and very much demonstrated especially when India or Pakistan are in the ascendancy.

On these occasions it is felt that 'local' Indians identify with people of the same origin, assert their 'roots' and demonstrate pride in it. This reflects a lack of loyalty and national pride for the country of their birth. The 'tragic' outcome of this is the perception held by the non-Indian populace that all Indians are supportive of the teams which hail from the motherland and are therefore viewed with suspicion whatever their loyalties might be. In reality there is a great proportion of cricket-loving Indians whose loyalties are fixed, constant and embedded in the Caribbean. There is a climate of tension prevailing during these visits. This was clearly seen, in that 1971 series when India was image-making and receiving overt support from its local Indian contingent.

This divided loyalty and lack of national spirit together with the problem of inter-island rivalry in the selection of players for the region, need to be further addressed by the critics. Hilary Beckles in a spirit of optimism sees the game in the West Indies as the beacon of nationalism and unity and C.L.R.James envisaged it as the most assimilating force in the life of the Caribbean people. But in light of the divisiveness which is evident, more so in the 1990s, it is wise to reflect now on our sense of nationalism with the hope and aim of fostering sincere solidarity among the Caribbean people.

In the final Test the stage was set for an entertaining and suspenseful duel between both teams. West Indies summoned their arsenal which included a wealth of bowlers and batsmen capable of performing both roles or duties, expressly determined in their quest for victory. A positive Sobers, a great fighter, who at times assumed the mantle of opening bowler was capable through his versatility, of changing his bowling style in accordance with the demands of the game; in addition he was most agile and dependable in the slips. After his dismissal of Abid Ali, he was injured in a successful attempt to catch Wadekar; this forced a temporary retirement. India managed to reach 360 with Gavaskar contributing 124, another century. The innings was shaped around him; he took charge of it and fashioned it. With the exception of Sardesai, 75, and Venkataraghavan he had no sustained support. But this achievement was not without its agonizing frustration of enduring physical pain, excruciating and almost sinister. To face pace bowling in hot tropical sun with an almost intolerable tooth ache demands courage and inner strength.

Without such qualities an individual is likely to be plunged into a state of depression. The occasion tested the strength of his character, sense of endurance, resilience, qualities which this batsman did epitomize.

Brunell Jones vividly recalls Gavaskar's dominance and imposing presence at the crease:

"Sunil Gavaskar took complete control of his team's second innings after India had lost Abid Ali when the score was 11. He dominated a second wicket stand with Wadekar, during which they took the total to 159. Foster held a red-hot return from Sardesai at 194 and Sobers knocked away Vishwanath's stumps and bails when the little man was on the borderline of what looked like a big score.

But Gavaskar, solid, hawk-eyed, compact and confident, went right on, punishing Dowe, Sobers, Holford, Noreiga and Shepherd. He won the first of a large collection of garlands and kisses from the spirit-of-youth spectators when he reached his second century of the match and thereafter, as he crossed milestone after milestone, play was held up. The hero-worshippers ... bless them; they brought fresh, healthy and colourful winds of change to a sport which seems to be in danger of extinction... were almost free from molestation by 'guardians of the peace', as they ran onto the field to kiss and hug their 'partner' ."

During the course of his second innings Gavaskar continued to experience the torment of pain intensified by weakness and sleepless nights, but he was inspired through sheer dedication to steer India to safety. This innings here of a double century was an epic one; it was an attractive sequel after his single century in the first innings and evinced the extraordinary mettle which characterized his career; glimpses of which were recognized during his childhood cricket.

The climate, the brilliant sunshine, the morning "all bright and glittering in the smokeless air" established the mood for an in-form batsman. His innings grew and flourished as if he were touched by the beauty of the scene; it was this condition of spirit which nullified his pain and determined his dynamism at the crease.

Gavaskar's dominance was emphatic and insistent throughout the innings. In Keatsian terms, he set about to "load and bless" his batting with a variety of strokeplay, controlling the variety of bowling styles he encountered. His strokeplay was an expression of faithfulness to his craft as a batsman, the development of craft we were to witness later in his career. Here was a great innings, not structurally careless, not fragmented, but well-crafted and disciplined, shaped into a smoothly moulded work of art. He recalls when he reached his 200 mark:

"Eventually, I reached the 200 run mark with a cover drive off Dowe. This brought about a virtual 'explosion' in the stands. The spectators surged on to the ground in their hundreds to congratulate me. One of the Indians even shoved the National flag in my hand. I was hoisted on willing shoulders as the frenzied spectators danced about with me in joy. It was all very moving, and I shall never forget those few exciting moments on a foreign field far away from home. However, I was scared that, in their enthusiasm, my admirers might pull an arm or a leg apart because quite honestly, the chaps were not in their senses. And if anybody by mistake even lightly bruised my jaw I would have been in trouble."

For eight hours and fifty minutes Gavaskar assumed command. His double century which followed his first innings century made him the second batsman to achieve such a feat. Doug Walters had scored 242 and 103 at Sydney against the West Indies in the 1968-69 season. This feat was later achieved by Lawrence Rowe and Greg Chappell.

Michael Manley who witnessed this magnificent display expressed his admiration in "Cricket Life" in November 1989. Of Gavaskar he writes:

"He had the perfect defence of the classic opening batsman. The driving was immaculate, left leg to the pitch of the ball,

the arc of the swing perfect, the follow-through sweet".
In simple and lucid description he continues:
"Throughout the magnificent double century, he never slashed outside the off-stump nor swung with abandon outside the leg stump. When he cut he was on top of the ball and obviously preferred forcing through mid-wicket, with the controlled use of his wrist, to the more dangerous business of sweeping."

Eric Williams, the late former Prime Minister of Trinidad, and a cricket enthusiast, who followed the game keenly, was also a witness to this memorable double-century. This performance and consistency of Gavaskar led Williams to proclaim him a batting genius.

With Gavaskar's contribution, the West Indies were faced with the task of achieving victory in 2 1/2 hours with a target of 212 runs. The drama was far from the end for the Indians final sally almost earned them victory. At the conclusion of play, West Indies were fighting to stave off defeat at 165 for 8. The final outcome was a drawn Test but an Indian victory for the first time, historic and imperishable; it was an annihilation mainly through Gavaskar and who, though in utter pain and agony, forged a new destiny for his country's cricket.

Gavaskar demonstrated a combative energy which seemed inexhaustible, an immensity of effort and endurance, irrepressible youth against the hostility of pace. The magic of 1971 lingers on and the echoes of the bugles which blow his song are not the Tennysonian dying echoes but imperishable and permanent. He did "surprise by a fine excess", a surfeit that never sickened nor died but inspired greater appetite for success. He had enriched the series with a wealth of high scores, brilliant stroke play, gusto, dynamism, richness and variety. His beginning at the Oval was not deceptive for his innings flourished and blossomed and matured unlike the many who graced the turf with great promise and dramatic flair, but who sank into oblivion with an equally rapid departure.

The critics, though impressed, wondered whether this

accomplishment was merely a temporary elevation and looked towards his future career. Was his dramatic display a fleeting illusion or a foretaste of historic achievements to follow? Was it the beginning of a career which would eventually stand up to scrutiny?

With the series at an end there was a clear appreciation and fuller recognition of Gavaskar's sense of daring and the quality of his craft; here was an exhibition of skill and technique which appealed to the imagination of the spectators. The West Indians saw it as the birth of a 'terrible beauty'.

In an effort to capture the spirit which pervaded, Lord Relator, a Trinidadian calypsonian, was moved to celebrate India's achievement in song...particularly the feats of Gavaskar. The lyrics in printed form tell the story:

> *It was Gavaskar*
> *the real master*
> *Just like a wall*
> *we couldn't out Gavaskar at all*
> *not at all*
> *you know the West Indies couldn't*
> *out Gavaskar at all.*

But the mood, feeling, spontaneity can only be experienced in the rendition of the song in its entirety. The full lyric, its measured rhythms make great impact and the lines are memorable.

In terms of records the following indicates his achievement during his first series - His aggregate of 774 is the highest in a maiden Test series. Before this, George Headley held the record of 703 in 1929-30 against England.
- His century and double century feat in one Test was achieved only by K. D. Walters before him. Later Lawrence Rowe and Greg Chappell were to achieve it.
- Everton Weekes aggregate of 779 was the highest in a series between India and the West Indies. Gavaskar's 774 was 5 short of Weekes' but he achieved it in only four Test matches.

- His average of 154.80 stands out as one of the more impressive ones in Test Cricket. But there are higher averages, for example, Don Bradman's 201.50 and 178.75.

Another game, another series had concluded; a defeat for the West Indies but a historic triumph for India in their ascendancy, a bright flicker to kindle their spirit to greater commitment, to excellence and ultimately greater self-esteem. A series had come to an end but it was a time to re-examine our cricketing selves in the Caribbean and a time for Indian rejoicing and solidarity.

What I envisaged here was the human spirit, agitated by historical cricketing catastrophes of previous tours, now asserting itself, soaring with confidence and returning home in triumph, a victory purifying and cathartic; an inspired India in the spirit of greater competitiveness and accomplishment, towards the continuing health of the game. Indeed the cricketers did cherish on their return to their country, the sound of revelry and the music with its voluptuous swell, indicators of the solidarity and wholeness of a country in its precious moments.

CHAPTER 2

The Early Years

..................The passion yet
was in its birth, sustained as might befall
By nourishment that came unsought.

William Wordsworth: The Prelude

H ad the mystics and gurus been present at Sunil Gavaskar's birth, they would certainly have proclaimed that Providence saw to it his well-defined identity mark was one of greatness, that he was indeed ear-marked for greatness. This was evident 21 years later, when he experienced his finest hour at Queen's Park Oval only to be followed by increasing hours of heroic performances.

The narration of his birth and the circumstances surrounding it is rendered by Sunil Gavaskar in his early autobiography "Sunny Days":

"I may never have become a cricketer and this book may never have been written, if an eagle-eyed relation, Mr. Narayan Masurekar, had not come into my life the day I was born (July 10,1949). It seems that Nan-Kaka (as I call him), who had come to see me in hospital on my first day in this world, noticed a little hole near the top of my left ear lobe. The next day he came again and picked up the baby lying on the crib next to my mother. To his utter horror, he discovered that the baby did not have the hole on his left ear lobe. A frantic search of all the cribs in the hospital followed, and I was eventually located sleeping blissfully beside a fisherwoman, totally oblivious of the commotion I had caused! The mix-up, it appears, followed after the babies had been given their bath.

Providence had helped me to retain my true identity, and in the process, charted the course of my life. I have often

19

wondered what would have happened if nature had not 'marked' me out, and given me my 'guard' by giving me that small hole on my left ear lobe; and if Nan-Kaka had not noticed this abnormality. Perhaps, I would have grown up to be an obscure fisherman, toiling somewhere along the West Coast. And, what about the baby, who, for a spell, took my place? I do not know if he is interested in cricket, or whether he will ever read this book. I can only hope that, if he does, he will start taking a little more interest in Sunil Gavaskar."

At the age of 38, the age of his retirement from active cricket, Gavaskar had spent 17 years devoted to cricket at its highest level. He had grown from the school boy cricketer, to club, university and first class levels and ultimately to Test class cricket. During these years his achievements ranged from university graduate, writer of cricket books, mainly autobiographical, sports columnist, cricket commentator, agent of endorsements and advertisements, social worker, business executive to a cricketing great. His career encompassed a range and diversity of activities unknown to many who know him only as a great opening batsman with a record of 34 centuries and the first batsman to accomplish the feat of acquiring over 10,000 runs. It is necessary to examine his stages of achievements, not only as a batsman whose skills were used to counter bowling attacks but in the conventional terms of biography, to trace his early development to his emergence as a central figure, dynamic and influential.

Born on July 10, 1949 in Bombay of the father Manohar Keshwar Gavaskar and the mother Meenal Gavaskar formerly Mantri, Sunil Gavaskar, a Hindu by religion of the Grand Saraswat Brahmin Caste, lived in a moderately middle-class home; his was an enlightened home for his father was a Bombay University graduate in Economics and his mother also a Bachelor of Arts graduate. This educational background is of great significance for the sound development of any child and in this, the child Sunil was very fortunate, even more so as his mother was at home as his constant companion. He enjoyed the company and comfort of two sisters, Nutan, who now works with the national Air Line, Air India, and Kavita now married to one of India's famous cricketers, G.R. Vishwanath. His crowning family achievement was his marriage to Marshniel (Pammi) Mehrotra, educated, intelligent and graceful, who bore a son, Rohan, now a young college student.

Sunil's childhood days revealed a passionate obsession with the game of cricket. Perhaps, and it is only rational to think that this yearning and extraordinary burning desire derived from his father who was a school and club cricketer. Though his father missed playing for Bombay University, his interest in the game was lifelike and intense. In his father's company there was considerable exposure and this instilled love and fascination for the game.

His mother came from a family with a keen interest in cricket; her brother Madhav Mantri, was a regular player in the Ranji trophy tournaments and represented India in four Test matches. At his tender age, Sunil was fascinated and intrigued by the trophies, souvenirs, embellishments which adorned his uncle's home. These had all been won through cricketing achievements. Later, Gavaskar recalls when he requested pullovers from his uncle, he was told that he had to work towards getting his own. This he remembered very well and was happy that his uncle did not succumb to his wish. His uncle's response did not displease but inspired him to achieve through his own application and skill.

This passionate, intense love and unique interest in the game, he says, started when he was a child:
"At that time it meant everything to me. I thought, slept, lived cricket and only cricket."
During his early years he lived in a compound with a block of four buildings. Within the confines of this restricted area he would play with his mother who bowled him with a tennis ball for long periods. This restricted setting forced him to exercise control of his strokes; loose, careless and aggressive shots would endanger another's physical body or neighbour's

property and it did on occasions. His mother could bear testimony to that for she herself suffered once. There was virtue in the limitations placed on his batting and he realized while playing, his shots had to be disciplined and carefully executed.

This fanatical preoccupation led him into conflict with his neighbourhood friends with whom he played, many times showing a selfish desire to dominate with the bat.
"Right from the beginning, I wanted to become a batsman and I hated losing my wicket. This became such an obsession with me that, if the rest of the boys ever got me out, I would fight and eventually walk home with the bat and ball."
But when the squabbles were over fellowship prevailed. There were times when the boys were led to conspire against him in order to curtail his stay at the crease.

This fascination of playing for long hours, even with his mother, is not surprising in the light of his long sojourns at the crease in his Test career, the number of times he countered heroic bowling with patience, concentration and energy. This he did for his self-esteem and his country but not selfishly. This interest in cricket was nurtured and further developed with the company of boys whose participation allowed for his continuing exposure and experience. They were always arranging competitions, rewarding players for their successes with small metal cups as trophies, congratulating themselves with measured spoons of lemonade and savouring them. This was cherished much more than all the extravagant profligate excess of champagne which is either consumed or spilled during the excited jubilation which follows Test victory.

Montessori school was his first exposure to 'formal' education and this was supported tremendously by a mother, gentle, soft-spoken, of mature calm, of high moral principles of honesty and truth; a woman with courage of conviction however soft she appeared, qualities which he imbibed for he was able during his career to articulate his convictions once he felt strongly. Nor was his exposure at school confined to the fundamentals of reading and writing but also to singing, drama, impersonation of characters in which he actively participated.

At home, religious experience was not denied, though the family did not actively participate in big prayers and poojas. There was silent devotion and scope for spiritual development through teachings of the basic tenets, through didactic approach or through religious and mythical stories which his mother read to him. This consciousness was reflected when he immediately retired to the prayer room on hearing of his selection to Test cricket. Through her constant presence during these early years, she was able to instil a keen sense of discipline and desirable human qualities. His upbringing did nurture in him a sense of care and consideration for others. During his humble beginnings he showed compassion for people who were in need and would always lean on his mother to assist the indigent. Later during his heyday and amidst the glitter and glamour he took time to attend to others who needed some form of sustenance. Based on the strength of his altruism and accomplishment and his compassion, his mother was inspired to write a work in Marathi which is entitled "The Ideal Son".

Interest in cricket never waned. At St. Xavier's High School he was of age to develop his skill and receive or summon greater support from teachers who became conscious of and alert to his dedication to the game. Here he would participate in inter-class matches on weekends without the trappings of sophisticated cricket equipment and gear. As his cricket continued and progressed positively, he was motivated by his sisters and parents, even receiving financial rewards for outstanding batting performances.

His father emphasizes that his career did not develop by chance or accident; it was a hobby for him and he kept excelling with practice and keen, intense observation of senior players. From about the age of 12 years he would accompany his father on weekends to the Cross Maidan or the Azad Maidan to look at cricket matches. This he did with utmost concentration, interest and pleasure. His father, though not actively involved in his son's educational pursuits, for he was a working man, saw to it together with his wife that Sunil's educational career was not wasted, that there was an acceptable blend of school and sporting interest, that the pleasure of cricket and the useful acquisition of knowledge and education were preserved.

During Sunil's final year at high school, he was selected for a camp organized at Hyderabad under the guidance of T.S. Worthington, a former English player. There he was exposed to the rudiments of the game, especially with an English flavour. But he never really subscribed to the rigid, formal coaching exhibitions; his development grew out of keen observation, experimentation, practice and the advice of his father, which was of considerable value to him. Of his father, he says:
"....... we have interesting discussions on various aspects of the game, and I have found his advice invaluable in the development of my career."
His gratitude was later expressed when he made his first Test century in Guyana.

One of Sunil's childhood friends who shared a long ingrafted relationship with him, Milind Rege, always recalls their pleasures and disappointments of playing cricket and marble games, but what impressed Milind was Sunil's amazing powers of concentration; this was his greatest asset. His batting talent was sensational; his drives, hooks, cuts seemed to be spawned from the bat.

Among his friends both at school and home he was respected for his forthright stand when the circumstance demanded it or he was at times tolerant of his friends' infirmities as they were of his imperfections. Such incidents are too innumerable to recall and indeed improbable to narrate in this work. But their pastimes and recreational activities, though not of the verdant village greens of Blunden's English country or the Wordsworthian winding cataracts, were filled with pleasure, so gleeful and rapturous and enchanting, that they heeded not the summons for early evening retirement.

With a youthful imagination captured and enthused by the game, the joy of batting was an incentive to him, his ability to play the ball stylishly, to counter the bowling as a conquest, defend his wicket with honour. It was an individual victory, a triumph of his craft with the same pleasure the writer derives from use of language, or the sculptor from his carving. The triumphs he experienced increased his passion for and devotion to the game.

One of his friends, Leander Dias, recalls an incident as recently as 1994 in which Sunil, though in retirement, further revealed his divine devotion to the game and his craft. Dias faithfully describes a collision between Sunil and a little boy which resulted in the boy's bat falling to the ground. Sunil requested that the boy rest it on the ground after which he took it up himself, kissed it and then returned it to the boy. It is the quality of respect or reverence which amazes.

Such was his dedication to the game that he was determined to improve his fielding which was not of acceptable cricketing standard. This he did until he eventually became a good close fielder in the slips at Test level, so much so that, during the Rest of the World vs Australia championship in 1972, he won the award for best fielding.

Though he possessed the ability to bat and powers of concentration from an early age, his initiation into competitive school cricket in the Giles and Harris shield tournament was not encouraging, failing in batting and fielding. In fact Sunil experienced the torment of frustration on his climb up the cricketing ladder; failure, doubts, frustrating performances during his career up to the Ranji Trophy level, plagued him; but with undaunted spirit and courage, he persevered.

S. Sivaramakrishnan, in his doctoral thesis on Gavaskar, notes of his successes at high school level:

"The academic years 1965-66 proved to be the best when he scored four hundreds in the Senior Inter-School matches for the Harris Shield. In the All India tournament for the Cooch-Behar Trophy in that year, he totalled 760 runs averaging 152.00. He created a record with a first wicket partnership of 421 runs making an individual contribution of 246 not out. He scored 222 runs in the semi finals against East Zone schools and made 85 against North Zone in the finals. He was awarded the J.C. Mukherjee Trophy for the 'best school-boy cricketer of the year', being the first prize in a national competition. This notable performance got him selected to represent the All India schools' team against London School Boys who were touring India. He played in the first four Tests against London Schools and scored an aggregate of 309 runs."

This spate of run-scoring with its high scores simply indicated to his peers and administrators of the game his rare qualities of concentration and skill. His insatiable appetite for enormous scores continued and he developed into a prolific scorer at Test level.

Sunil's educational pursuits did not suffer at the expense of his cricket. He entered St. Xavier's College in 1966 to pursue higher education and while reading for his degree with a major in special economics, he saw to it that his cricket was not neglected. Representing his college in the Inter-Collegiate tournament of 1966 he put on a first wicket partnership of 472 with Ramesh Nagdev; his contribution was 209. After consistent batting form he was selected on the Bombay University team. Prolific scores streamed from his willow. In the Inter-University tournament for the Robinton Baria Trophy of 1966-67, he scored 106 against Jabalpur and 139 not out against Baroda. His 247 not out against South Zone universities was the highest individual record in the Vizzy Trophy, the inter-university tournament. This was followed by an innings of 113 not out in the finals against North Zone in 1968-69 season. When he scored over 200 for Bombay University in another inter-university match and then threw away his wicket, he was criticized by his Uncle Mantri for reckless waste of his wicket. The lesson here was that he should never surrender to the bowler. It is interesting to recall here an incident in which Ranjitsinjhi (of Indian origin but who played for England), a batsman of renowned distinction in England was pleasantly displeased by his nephew K.S. Duleepsinjhi's (another Indian who played for England) reckless stroke in a Test match after he had scored 173. For this impetuous display Ranji cautioned his nephew "You should get your first hundred for the side, the next you get for the side, and then you may get one for yourself."

Very much conscious of his family's pride in his achievement he found inspiration. In a later match he had been encouraged by his mother to eclipse the 324 run record which was the highest contribution at University level made by Ajit Wadekar. This he did , scoring 327 runs; a record which still stands as a great tribute to his mother.

The coveted place in a Bombay state game in the Ranji Trophy tournament was his great ambition, but so far it had eluded him. For him it was disappointing and disturbing. After his performance against North Zone he anticipated a place in the Bombay XI but it was to no avail; yet he expressed determination to assert his claim. His pride, his dignity, his belief in his ability were the incentives which motivated him to think positively. In the Purshottan Shield final at Bombay he scored 301 not out but still the Ranji selectors were unmoved. Complacency never set in nor was his vision ever blinded to the conditions to which players were subjected. Though not as vocal as when he played at Test level, he was critical of the treatment meted out to players at university level; students should 'be treated as an investment for the future' and therefore 'the climate for the proper development of talent' must be created.

University level cricket experience was complemented by his Dadar Union Club commitments and this commitment he felt strongly; it was a club with a tradition for excellent fielding, discipline, tenacity and ability to fight back. It is no wonder that he felt such attachment and loyalty to Dadar. To him it was a 'dream side' which had established itself through the astute leadership of Madhav Mantri and Vasu Paranjpe, dynamic and capable. It was Vasu who gave Sunil his abbreviated name 'Sunny' as he is now popularly known.

Gavaskar has written about his admiration for P.K. Joe Kamat and Vithal M.S.Patil. Of Patil in particular he owes a debt of gratitude for the deep interest he took in him, unwavering moral support in addition to his assistance on the field. With swing bowling almost unplayable, Patil would bowl to aspiring cricketers, discover their faults, chinks in their armour, and help to correct them. Patil, he found, was insightful and showed confidence in him.

A period of sterility stepped in and he found difficulty in scoring both at university and at club level but surprisingly after what he deemed a barren season with only few purple patches he was selected for the 1970 Bombay team in the Ranji Trophy Tournament. Against Mysore, he was dismissed for a duck in the first over and managed a meagre 27 not out in the second innings. The crowd's response to his first Bombay XI appearance was negative and made life agonizing for him. The perception was that his selection was an act of nepotism since his uncle Madhav Mantri, was a member of the selection panel. It was learnt later that Mantri never ventured an opinion when it came to Sunil's selection.

The match which followed against Rajasthan gave him one more chance to prove his mettle. With a huge opening partnership of 279 of which he managed 114, Gavaskar's confidence soared and was further encouraged by the supportive Raj Singh Dungarpur and Hanumant Singh. It cleared the gloom and let the sunshine in. Here was an indication of the courageous fighting spirit of a youth asserting his desire to counter adversity. It was one of the many instances which later characterized him; he never allowed failure to deter his quest and this was the basis of his success.

In 1970 he was selected vice-captain of the Indian Universities in its tour against Sri Lanka University. Here a prolific 203 was then followed on his return home by a century for Bombay against Gujurat in the Ranji Trophy and then 176, another Ranji Trophy century. His career began to blossom and his reputation had to be preserved.

At this time, a tour to the West Indies was approaching and all attention was focussed on this series. There were those who gave him support and encouragement and hoped for his selection on the Indian team; but he remained pessimistic; for him only a few first-class matches to his credit was no reason for optimism; but then , he had scored three consecutive centuries. Anxiety and suspense filled the air around and this did not ease the tension he experienced in his anticipation of a place on the team to tour the Caribbean.

To his great surprise it did come:

"I felt a tremendous surge of happiness and hugged my parents, who were shedding tears of joy. I immediately went to the room in which the daily prayer is performed and prayed for the Almighty's blessings."

A new opportunity, a most coveted one lay ahead; he was moving from a past fraught with dedication and intense participation in the game; it was a past with a fair measure of achievement or success. His domestic career to this point was not without its agony and frustration. Later in his career he would continue to experience anguish and dejection which at times accompany or attend success. But now it was for him, a new beginning; it was a new phase, for he was about to enter 'fresh woods and pastures new'. So to the Caribbean he journeyed, not knowing of the dramatic encounter in the distance.

CHAPTER 3

Years Of Awakening

But I have straightened out
Ruin, wreck and wrack
I toiled long years and at length
came to so deep a thought
I can summon back
All their wholesome strength.

W.B. Yeats: The Results of Thought

The summer luxury of the Caribbean tour in 1971 with its display of fine excess was recorded for posterity in the cricket hall of fame, and a cricketing career lay ahead of Sunil. The euphoria and festivity which enthralled India was no longer visibly demonstrated, but the memory of it lingered on. The team's major preoccupation was the visit to England in the middle of 1971. Gavaskar, known for his extraordinary feat, was placed on a pedestal and this meant that expectations for continued successes were high. How would he face the challenge ahead? This was the burning issue that faced him.

The critics argued and wondered whether his prolific form would be sustained. The emotionally charged supporters envisaged a hero championing India's cricket destiny in different lands; the more rational and mature expressed the view that it was not humanly possible to re-enact the scene or re-create such feats unabatedly, however much they desired it.

As it turned out, the history records revealed that the few years between 1971-75 were a period of awakening; some call them years of apprenticeship. For him it was an awakening to the unpredictable realities of sporting life, a life with the varying forces of success and failure, glory and despair. For a figure in the public eye, success is exhilarating and beatific; failure could be terrifying and agonizing. The years which faced Gavaskar were years of learning and development but not without despair and anguish; periods of uncertainty and demanding challenges. In the process, he was maturing into a fully recognized international player. The poet Yeats was preoccupied with the struggle with words; to express with precision and compactness the complexity of his stream of thought and emotion was an exacting and difficult process; for Sunil the struggle with his craft, perfecting it against the diversity of opponent and conditions of play engrossed him but the fascination of the difficult challenge never dried the sap out of his veins; he had the rare ability to survive amidst adversity, a strong test of his strength of character and fortitude.

Before the advent of the 1971 tour to the West Indies no credit was given to India's stature; in fact past years of cricketing experience expressed a story of mediocrity. The English shared the West Indian's perception of India's place in world cricket. The English, very visibly, through their wide arsenal of tabloids, were very punitive in their criticism of India's talent, the talent of 'children of a lesser God'. Their criticism had ranged from amused irony to outright condemnation. Tours to India were frowned upon. Players perceived visits as drudgery and many made themselves unavailable.

The files of history reveal that the encounters between both teams over the years proved English superiority. India's performance at home was not as dismal as abroad. The 37 Test matches played yielded three wins for India, 16 drawn and 18 lost games. India triumphed at home on three occasions but there were no successes in England, the records reading 4 drawn and 15 lost games.

But in 1971 India's sense of optimism was reassuring and such mood and spirit were conducive to creditable performances. Gavaskar described their spirit as 'fighting fit.' It must be noted that in 1971 the English were enjoying the pleasures of a prolonged succession of victories. With an impressive record of 23 victories including the recapture of the Ashes from Australia, the English were also in high spirits and eagerly awaited an encounter with the new emerging talented Indian team. India shared some measure of hope after England's narrow victory against Pakistan for this margin of victory indicated that English superiority was not unrestrained, that the English could be contained.

With both teams poised for an encounter, the English eyes were focussed on Gavaskar and the marvellous image portrayed through his recent prodigious presence. For him it meant greater stress and tension. It was also an introduction to new conditions; he was more familiar and at home with the climatic conditions and batting strips in the Caribbean than with those in England. Gavaskar recalls the early performances of the batsmen which were encouraging.... Vishwanath, Wadekar, Sardesai, Mankad and himself striking it profusely. But he was dismayed by the Lord's pitch and could not understand why cricketers are overawed by Lord's. Time and again he would be critical of the rigid formality of the upper echelons in the cricket fraternity at Lord's and in England in general.

In the first Test at Lord's, England marshalled their forces under Ray Illingworth, a well-balanced combination of batting and bowling to match India's sprightly team of performers. It was a match in which Sunil's innings never inspired for his scores of 4 and 53 were merely an initiation into Test cricket on England's hallowed grounds, a place where success eluded him throughout his career, but which yielded to his monumental presence during the Bicentenary celebrations in 1987. On that occasion he was among the most distinguished of world cricketers and like a true hero he emerged *primus inter pares*. The match itself here in 1971 was well-poised even in the last few hours but ended in an interesting drawn game. Though it ended inconclusively, it was punctuated by a dramatic and ugly incident in which Sunil and paceman John Snow were the main characters. It eventually was called the Snow Incident, the most controversial of the 1971 season.

Sunil reveals the minute but significant details of the incident in his book 'Sunny Days':

"Earlier during our partnership, just before lunch, an incident, the famous 'Snow charge', took place involving me. Snow bowled to Farokh from the Nursery End, and Farokh trying to turn a ball to leg missed and was hit on the thigh and the ball fell near short square-leg. We set off for a quick run. From the corner of my eye I saw Snow also setting off for the ball. I would have reached 'home' safely as Snow had gone across to the other side on his follow through. However, I found to my surprise that he was level with me and, with the ball nowhere near him, the hefty fast bowler gave me a violent shove, which sent me sprawling. Now, Snow is a well-built bowler, with strong shoulders, so that poor little me had no chance! I crawled to the crease having lost my bat in the tumble. Snow came and tossed the bat back to me. He did not fling it as reported in the newspapers. In fact, after lunch he came to me and apologised. However, the England selectors dropped him from the next Test as a disciplinary measure."

Gavaskar felt that the whole incident was overcharged with emotional outburst from the English critics and spectators. It was over-magnified. He had understood the bowler's plight at that particular time; anxiety and fear of defeat clouded Snow's rational thinking. Sunil never encouraged escalation of what to the English was unsavoury conduct; in fact he underplayed it and discussed it rather discreetly. His reaction emphasized his growing maturity and genial temperament in the midst of tension and uproar; his was a generous appraisal of the situation, one borne out of an awareness of man's frailty as a human condition, inevitable and predictable in moments of despair.

At this point, it is interesting to explore Tony Greig's interpretation of the incident, for he was playing in that match. Greig begins his account by saying:

"As Gavaskar set off for a short single, Snowy dashed to pick up the ball. Their paths crossed, and at the point of collision,

John dropped his shoulder, knocking the little Indian to the ground. Now there is no doubt in my mind that John did bump Gavaskar and that what he did was wrong. But I cannot agree with those who said that the barge was vicious."

Greig then raises the question of right of way. Is it the batsman or the bowler who has priority when the batsman is scuttling down the wicket and the bowler needs to get round him to the ball for a run-out attempt? In his view he strongly thinks that the bowler has right of way and in this incident Snow's action was mainly a sign of "frustration at being balked as he went for the ball."

After the collision, Snow then picked up the bat and tossed it back to Sunil. There are those who accuse Snow of throwing the bat at the batsman. This Greig refutes and is of the belief that Snow just lobbed the bat to Gavaskar in a gesture of apology.

The media in its consistent *modus operandi* dramatized the incident, re-enacting it on film in slow motion for the country to digest, and the newspapers articulated its reactions to Snow in "heavily couched terms".

If Snow's incident was a rude awakening, then in Sunil's eyes the umpiring decisions were appalling. He was dissatisfied with the arbiters of the game when he found umpiring decisions absurd. He was now being initiated into the nightmare experience of seeing poor and sometimes unfair umpiring decisions affecting crucially the outcome of games. It made him ponder on the integrity of arbiters of the game; in this particular case he found Umpire Constant consistently constant in his negative umpiring, turning decisions against India.

During the second Test, rain was the demon and eventually nulled all efforts England may have made to reap success. On the strength of scores, England were in the ascendancy and victory was in sight but rain intervened on India's behalf. It was felt that India were enjoying the fortune of not having lost at this stage but if we are charitable to them we will remember that weather conditions conspired against their spin attack as Bedi, Venkataragavan and Chandrasekhar experienced the frustration of using a wet slippery ball. Sunil himself was rather lucky to hold three catches in the first innings, a great incentive and boost to his confidence on the field.

It must be mentioned here that though England may have won, Sunil was disturbed by the decision in Illingworth's favour, one which to him was the turning point in the match. A straightforward bat and pad catch by Solkar off Chandrasekhar was disallowed. Sunil says "it was the third time in three innings that Illingworth had been given a second life by the umpires. I guess there are advantages to being an English captain in England."

Illingworth made use of this opportunity and went on to score a century. In doing so he added 168 runs with Peter Lever to put England in a commanding position. Sunil was not impressed; his idealism, as a young man did not fit into the scheme of things. This he would experience as his career progressed. The game, though affording opportunities for personal glory and assertion of national pride, also was fraught with the harsh realities on and off the field. He became a central figure later on for he was yet to experience decisions that affected him personally, decisions that went for him, much to the wrath of the opponents, or decisions that went against him. His sense of idealism would not only be ruffled by the realities of umpiring decisions but other significant matters and events which we shall explore later.

In response to England's innings at Old Trafford, India faced the brunt of the inhospitable weather and the pace of Lever and Price. It is meaningful to remember that Sunil's innings of 57 here was a true expression of the character emerging in the face of adverse conditions. He recalls that this innings was the most challenging of his career. He wore no helmet and the temperature was not encouraging when Price and Lever used the conditions to full advantage. Of this Sunil vividly recalls:

"The over that Price bowled to me and got my wicket was the fastest spell of fast bowling I've ever faced."

Later he made a comparison with Thomson's pace in 1977: "I faced all the quicks in my career, but the only one who came close to Price that day was Jeff Thomson in Perth in December 1977. That pitch was quicker anyway, but Thomson bowled faster at me than he ever did before."

Sunil, later in 1974 on a revisit to England scored a century at Old Trafford, an innings he considered the best century of his career.

The third Test at the Oval was decisive. Through Chandrasekhar's guile with bowling figures of 6 for 38, India were in a position to force victory and this was eventually achieved. For Sunil the match was not a great personal success but it was a historic achievement for the team, their first victory for India in England and also a victory in the series. India were now in the forefront; it was unofficially hailed as the new cricketing champions, a claim which they still had to justify. As in the West Indies, it was a triumph for Indian cricket and its team spirit, so too in England, India's competitiveness and combative spirit was evident. Though she had entered England with a modicum of respect after the Caribbean tour, England's stature was imposing and she would not allow herself to be easily demoralized.

For Sunil the tour was an educational experience; he was forced to make adjustments to new and dreadful climatic changes, to a variety of bowling styles and was expected to cope responsibly with his task as an opener. It was a challenge he accepted and with credit he performed though not in the gallant style which characterized his Caribbean batting. There was not the surfeit of runs of the first tour but his competence in England was recognized.

This recognition was further evidenced when he was selected for the Rest of the World XI against Australia after the England tour. It was a most cherished opportunity to meet distinguished players from all the cricketing countries, current players and former greats including Don Bradman. Sunil was impressed with the remarkable composure and charm of the veteran who was most engaging during their first encounter. In response to Gary Sobers' affectionate provocation Bradman said to Sunil, "These big blokes have the power, but we little ones have the footwork."

The Don was supportive and encouraging, and at his age demonstrated a keenness of observation when he remarked on the beauty of a square drive Sunil had played in the South Australia match. He also instilled in Sunil that a judicious blend of attack and defence should be the hallmark of his batting style.

On this visit Sunil found Thomson erratic. Against him he was meeting the ball well and found the ball coming to the bat. Lillee's quality of pace earned the respect of all the batsmen. For him the series was no emphatic display of his talent but he was well pleased with his role as opener and he managed a few fifties, two of them in the Tests and his highest score on tour being 95. But more importantly he was witness to impressive innings from Sobers, Kanhai, Peter Pollock, Graham Pollock, Greg Chappell, Ian Chappell and Doug Walters. In one particular match he remarked of Kanhai:

"Watching him bat that day was an education on how to play pace bowling."

Kanhai's batting style and technique made a deep impression on Sunil. Such was his admiration that he named his son Rohan in appreciation of his respect for and friendship with Rohan Kanhai.

The sight of Sobers in full majesty was amazing to the young ambitious Sunil. In one of the innings he observed that "anything pitched up was driven past the bowler and anything pitched short was cut or hooked savagely."

This keenness of observation and critical examination of the diverse batting styles he witnessed was reminiscent of his boyhood days when he sat uncomplainingly and watchfully, feasting his eyes on cricket games in Bombay. The series was a harvest fulfilment, a festival of genuine cricket genius on display. It was fraught with rich and prolific innings which were expressive of elegance, sureness of touch, and gifted craftsmanship against bowling of unrelenting speed and versatility. Not on all occasions did the bat emerge victor in the contest, for the quality of bowling and its effectiveness were admirable features of the series. The experience of this series proved immensely rich in acquisition of knowledge and skills which the series brought to bear on him. In his development he showed great humility and a willingness to learn and adjust. Though he won the prize for best fielding he felt that Clive Lloyd's performance was most outstanding.

The series afforded the cricketers an opportunity to develop friendships and enjoy fellowship free from the tedium of intense rivalry. These experiences Sunil cherished; the interfacing with people of diverse cultural origins and backgrounds, and a sense of wholeness and solidarity made the tour and life more enjoyable and imperishable in the memory.

After fifteen months of rest from international cricket, India resumed battle with England but this time in India. In this series Sunil's performance in five innings yielded 60 runs..... 12 and 8, 18 and 2, 20 and 0. In the fourth and fifth Tests he restored some measure of respectability to his image. Here was a cricketer of great promise, faltering at the crease, not living up fully to the expectations of the home crowd. The struggle to create and build a respectable innings for his self-esteem and for his team which depended on him must have been traumatic. He recalls how he was heckled and felt embarrassed by their behaviour. It was the pressure of failure, of not achieving as anticipated, that unnerved him. But in his characteristic pattern he was able to endure the agonies and disappointments and respond by using his craft to advantage. This was demonstrated clearly when at Kanpur and Bombay, scenes of the fourth and fifth Tests, he scored half-centuries in each Test. Out of a total of 24 innings so far he had made

11 half centuries, quite a fair achievement though he did not blossom fully or live up to expectations. There was at least a measure of consistency and at his age there was promise of greater deeds. It is significant to note that during the fourth Test he had achieved the feat of scoring 1000 runs in Test cricket. He had made it in 11 Test matches; it was the fastest by an Indian batsman, but in his evaluation such an achievement should have come earlier since 774 of these were scored in four Tests. It took him seven more matches to score 226 in order to achieve the 1000 mark.

The critics were sympathetic in their analysis of his performance for they recognized that his successful debut was followed by an Australian tour, an English season and then domestic cricket. These could have put pressure on him, especially the tour matches. There were those who empathized with his recent performances but there were also some whose eyes were constantly fixed on him to see whether the sparkle of 1971 will ever be rekindled. In this context, Kanpur and Bombay were quite effective responses to the negative displays of the earlier Tests. It indicated that he was beginning to glow again and recapture his Test form. His aggregate, however, looked rather poor........ 224 runs at an average of 24.88.

It is also significant to note English criticism of Indian players and spectators during the 72-73 season. The English felt that Indian players were putting pressure on umpires to make decisions against England and they also complained about the preparation of wickets. Sunil was always alert to criticism and when convinced of his position, always had the courage to articulate his views. This he did simply and unequivocally. *"In India, the complaint is not only against the manner of our 'appealing' it is the condition of our wickets also. It is alleged that Indian wickets are invariably tailored for our spinners. True! Absolutely true! We would be fools if we did not prepare wickets to suit our ace spinners. When we go to England, we cannot distinguish the wicket from the outfield. And aren't English wickets prepared for the advantage of their own bowlers? But of course it is alright for England to do it. The British are fair but we are not."*

The series ended with Sunil showing signs of the old form, but only the 1974 series in England would indicate how progressive his career would be. But India's achievement was occasion for comfort; she had emerged victorious again and was more justified in her claim as world champions. Sunil, however, was reluctant to assert this claim without a contest with the Australians. Since there was no recent encounter between them, it was not a valid claim. This would only be seen in the 1977-78 tour.

India's encounters with England during the last two tours abroad and at home were a great inspiration. A resumption of the contest in 1974 was scheduled and the English smarting under defeat were determined to rescue their fortunes. With the determination which was part of his psyche, he pledged not to shave until he had added another century to his credentials. This came early for in the first Test at Old Trafford he achieved his goal. At this same ground he had scored 57 in 1971, an innings he remembers as among his best.

The series of 1974 tells a tale of misery, disappointment, conflict and anguish in the Indian camp. Dismal climatic conditions were an external reflection of the inner gloom, anguish and depression the team experienced. Even the sun conspired against India's hope; its presence was very occasional and when it appeared it dispelled the gloomy, grim conditions for a short period. Most of the Indians were not accustomed to the bitter cold and chill and they found the conditions unfavourable for good cricket.

Ashok Mankad, who enjoyed memorable occasions with Sunil felt that after his tours of the W.I. and England, Sunil simply had to progress. He felt that Sunil could not be reduced to mediocrity. In Sunil he saw the mettle of steel, one capable of doing yeoman service for his team. Mankad recalls Sunil's inner strength which propelled him to counter the assailant in an unflinching manner, bearing the pain like a great boxer who derives an enormous amount of pleasure after recovery from dealing the death blow. As an example of this 'warlike' attribute he cites one of Gavaskar's innings in the 1974 tour against Worcester. On a bitterly cold day, he looked on as Gavaskar countered Holder's attack. Holder at that time was genuinely fast and was formidable in conditions suited for fast bowling. The fourth ball of the first over was a tremendous blow to Gavaskar's rib cage but he never succumbed or surrendered, never showed pain, never divulged it to anyone. He returned next morning to resume battle with Holder and this debacle Mankad describes, as one of the greatest innings he had seen in 25 years. In that innings of 80 odd runs, 90 percent were made from Holder's bowling. Mankad recalls: "And in that knock there was everything that a connoisseur would like to see. Every kind of defensive technique, all the strokes, the cuts, the pulls, the glances. And the most edifying quality of it all....the triumph over his tormentor."

Only in recent times did Gavaskar show the impact zone of that blow which had remained blue and sore for over 15 days. In doing so he remarked:

"If I hadn't got that blow, I don't think I would have been able to play that innings, which is perhaps the best I have played."

It is reminiscent of the patience and determination he demonstrated so clearly in his epic innings at the Queen's Park Oval in 1971, though experiencing excruciating pain.

The other significant display of batting talent that made the tour an enhancing one for him and helped him gain confidence was his first Test at Old Trafford in 1974. It was a contest fought in cruel and unkind conditions; the bitter cold and the rain infested match intensified the batsman's misery. But the challenge of conquest, of mastering the conditions, however adverse, was his mission or even obsession. And his persistent and burning hope to restore the image which had been subjected to harsh critical language was foremost in his mind. He had arrived on the international scene as he says 'with a bang in 1971' and reflects that 'the period after was one of complete disappointment, to not only me but also for those who follow my cricket'. Both series against England lacked the flourishes people expected. He laments the poor performances.... a few fifties, no centuries. Gavaskar laments:

"And so people were already talking of the 1971 W.I. performance being just a flash in the pan."

If it were jubilation after his successes, then it was the wrath of ignominy after failure. To the skeptical and cynical, the West Indian attack of 1971 was friendly. Sobers was not challenging as a captain, chances were freely given. Conscious of this hostile criticism and in the midst of the 1973-74 bleak domestic season with failures in the Ranji Trophy, he was compelled to bring to his craft a new life and image.

Gerard Manley Hopkins favourite lines on the difficulty of creation in which he struggles to create poetry 'fresh and new' appropriately describe Gavaskar's predicament.

"Bird build but not I build
No, but strain times eunuch
and not breathe one work that wakes."

Blighted by unfavourable climatic conditions he summoned courage, though it was always difficult to score in England, he admits. At Old Trafford it was difficult to distinguish wicket from outfield. It was the greenest wicket he had encountered and hoped never to again. On this wicket he faced Bob Willis who was extremely quick; Chris Old had the seam at his command to do everything together with his short ones. The nagging accuracy of Mike Hendricks gave the batsman no great scope. Then there was Underwood whirling away "his quickish left arm spinners, pegging on the middle and leg, not letting you get even the singles."

Batting was an ordeal, and conquest under such conditions made his century here 'happier'. Sunil recalls:

"It broke my drought of centuries. I had not scored a century for three years. This century gave me the confidence that I

was capable of playing a long innings however significant, at Test level."

In this memorable innings the strokes that stand out vividly: *"A straight drive, and a short arm hook when Chris Old pitched one short and the ball firmly thudded into the fence; and an extra-cover drive off Mike Hendricks. These are the shots I recall with pleasure even now ten years after that hundred."* It was a resurgence, a new Sunil had come to the fore, but in spite of his masterful century and a good second innings score, England won the first Test, a result which Sunil felt was made easy for England through India's irresponsible batting.

In the second Test England started on a positive note. A total of 629 meant they were in a position to dictate the course of the match. India offered no resistance and therefore faced the follow-on. It was a most humiliating display of batsmanship in which India was demoralized scoring a paltry 42. This annihilation was decisive and only invited the media to further demoralize the spirit of the team. The London-based Indian journalists waged a serious campaign against the players, accusing them of in-fighting, drunkenness and a plethora of misdemeanours. Other dramatic incidents followed upon the defeat and the clash with journalists only made the situation unsavoury and full of rancour; it only created disintegration and loss of will and purpose among the players. This was further aggravated by an unfortunate scene of anger and bitterness between the High Commissioner and the team at his home; it was also over-dramatized by the press.

In the midst of this agonizing series, there was one incident which was most disturbing to Sunil. Sudhir Naik, a member of the team, had been accused of shop-lifting. In spite of the promise by the authorities to stifle the matter the news appeared in the press. For Gavaskar it was stressful and depressing. "I was shocked and was positive that this was all a mistake. I didn't ask him at all about what happened but later he told me and I had no doubt in my mind that he was innocent." This incident with Naik was most unfortunate since he was not given a chance to defend himself, but was deceived by the authorities at the store. He had gone to purchase toiletries and underwear at the store for himself and other players. It turned out that among his two pairs of trousers and twenty pairs of socks he had paid for , there were two additional pairs of socks . Before an explanation could be offered or the oversight handled discreetly, the salesgirl accused him of stealing.

Sunil felt that Naik was unfairly treated even in defense. He was annoyed with those concerned with giving him wrong advice. In defiance he says:

"The attitude of those concerned should have been 'to hell with the expenses, we'll go ahead and get our man a good lawyer for his defence."

Naik was not given a chance to defend himself and this meant that he was not able to clarify the issue, to clear doubts in the minds of people in England and at home. There was nothing that could have been done to repair the damage at that stage but to attempt to make conditions less stressful for Naik. Sunil therefore requested that Naik room with him for the rest of the tour. Though it was not the policy for players of the same State to share rooms, an exception was made. This gave Sunil the chance to bring some measure of calm to Naik's mental and emotional agony, an agony which even led him to contemplate suicide.

Sunil's role in this incident signals the quality of his humanity, the generosity of thought and consideration for others, especially in human situations where people are unfairly treated and innocently disgraced.

It tells of his sense of unfailing loyalty, a rare quality which many of his friends have lauded. His concern and care for others was expressed by Sandeep Patil who appreciated Sunil's humanity:

"I do not look to Sunil merely as a great cricketer. A friend and a guide and more than that our relations are still closer. After I established myself in Test cricket and some domestic problems threatened to overshadow my career, it was Sunil who acted as a friend, philosopher and guide and supported me through those lean and depressing moments."

It is with great pride that Hemant Waingankar, Milinde Rege, Leander Dias, Anil Joshi, Balan Sundaram and his senior mentors Raj Singh, Madhav Mantri, V.S.Patil speak of his respect for others, his loyalty and humility, qualities not infected by the glamour of his achievement.

This incident brings to mind Sunil's courage and strength, fearlessness and daring, even putting his life in jeopardy once convinced of a cause. I refer specifically to a violent scene, part of an uprising against a Muslim community, which Sunil witnessed from his apartment building. The report of January 31, 1993 which appeared in 'India Today' states:

"But a family of eight Muslims, whose car crashed on Worli Seaface after the driver was hit by a stone, were lucky. By the time the mob of youths reappeared with a fresh supply of stones to kill the bleeding victims, cricketer Sunil Gavaskar, who saw the attack from the balcony of his eight-floor apartment, rushed out, challenged the mob, and saved the family. They were taken to hospital in a police van."

To return to the tour of England, the Indians were again seriously humiliated at Birmingham; it was not only the team's failure but also a personal one. On reflection he says:

"It was a totally disastrous series and the tour was one of the worst I have made. There was no such thing as 'team spirit'. Instead there was a lot of petty squabbles, which didn't do anybody any good. The incidents which gave the team a bad name didn't help. It was all extremely frustrating."

Disastrous though the tour was, Sunil's further initiation into English conditions was useful for his career. Beyond the boundary, the complexities of life, its human and social foibles, trivia, the absurd, Sunil was able to understand with a breadth of outlook, a mature perception and generosity of spirit. The experiences felt and witnessed could only lead to personal enlightenment and development.

This tour had concluded and the 74-75 season would be brought to life with the approaching West Indian visit to India. Before this encounter, Sunil was intent on paying attention to his personal life in the form of matrimony. On September 23, 1974 he married Marshneil Mehrotra (Pammi), an event which he commented amusedly on:

"I was well and properly hooked." 'Hooked,' he recalls good-humouredly but not regretfully. For to this day Pammi has, through her strength of character and abiding faith, stood at his side in moments of disappointment and frustration, through the mire and complexity of a cricketing life with its periods of turbulence, conflict and anguish. These moments have not detracted significantly from the glorious forays which elevated him to cricketing stardom. Perhaps the perplexities and traumas added colour to a chequered career.

Defeat and low morale after the English tour was further compounded by the fickle, fluid, irresponsible crowd behaviour. There was a fanatic display of cruel behaviour and Wadekar was the main target. The concrete bat which had been erected at Indore in tribute to the 1971 victories over the West Indies and England was now defaced. Wadekar's house was stoned and there were demonstrations in front of his mother's house. The dramatic turn of events culminated in his exclusion from the West Zone team for the Duleep Trophy. This led to Wadekar's decision to retire from cricket, an end pre-mature but it further demonstrated the enigma of the Board's policies and decision-making procedures. To Sunil it was incredible. He felt that Wadekar's failure in the last tour may have warranted exclusion from the position of captaincy but, in Gavaskar's words, "To drop him from the side altogether was ridiculous." Sunil lamented the demise of Wadekar and in a positive statement gave an honest appraisal of Wadekar's role and contribution to Indian cricket. Very succinctly he says:

"Ajit Wadekar should be given the major credit for our emergence as a cricketing power. He got the best out of a talented lot of cricketers. In fact, he tapped the hidden potential of a lot

of cricketers in the team and got their seniors to contribute. The credit should go solely to him and our fielding, which improved beyond recognition during his captaincy."

The Indian's crowd fanaticism in most states is an intriguing feature of the game. Though they are in the periphery their part in the game is dominant. Sunil, later in his career would experience the joy and thrill of adulation and the wrath of their anger and perversity. Their passion for entertainment, if satisfied, would lead to extreme forms of hero-worship and respect. If however, their heroes faltered or through some imperfection do not delight and gratify their selfish pleasure, adulation would be transformed into utter denigration and ridicule, with the hero being reduced to the status of 'unaccommodated man'.

The West Indies tour to India was his second encounter with the Caribbean cricketers; on this occasion it was on home ground. He had been appointed to a new role, that of vice-captain, with Pataudi, who was recalled by the cricket board, as captain. Failure in the first Test did not daunt him and he experienced the delight at the prospect of leading India in the second Test due to Pataudi's injury. "When the news came, I was too stunned to believe it. Of course I had ambitions of leading India but I never expected it then. Imagine me as captain! I was in a sweet daze."

This was a sincere expression of excitement and joy. In matters of personal pride he would express himself with honesty of feeling and thought. In matters concerning his cricket and the welfare of the game he was never too reticent and expressed in an articulate manner his opinions and convictions, however disconcerting to others. On reflection, at the end of his career, he felt he could have been less rigid and more flexible with the Cricket Board.

The ecstatic mood paled into gloom when he was injured for the third time in the right index finger. The blow was both physical and mental for it meant a continual nagging pain and the frustration of not representing his country for three matches. The final Test at his home ground, Bombay, was some measure of relief for him. For this match he was all eager anticipation, especially in front of a crowd, knowledgeable and appreciative of the game; a crowd which to a great extent transcended the narrow provincialism and parochialism of crowd support. It was a crowd keen on the sport and its entertaining value but on this occasion, incensed by police brutality to an individual spectator, it expressed its anger through violence by destroying benches and fences and setting afire a section of the stadium.

Facing a West Indies imposing score of 604, India performed creditably to save the follow on with a reply of 406. Gavaskar's contribution of 86 in the first innings was satisfying to him for he had entered the Test with doubts about his fitness, having missed two months of first class cricket. West Indies eventually won this match and with it the series at 3-2. Though beaten at Bombay, India was not humiliated; it had fought back from 2-0 to level the series at 2-2 before the final encounter. Their performance in the series lifted the sagging morale which suffered tremendously during the 1974 English tour.

To this time in 1975, Sunil had played five series in Test cricket, participating in 17 matches. After the extraordinary feat in 1971 in the West Indies, his career showed mere glimpses of his batting skill. By no measure of criticism, did he fail, but he did fail to meet the expectations of the cricketing world. The critics described his performance after 1971 as moderate; he was still the young batsman with prowess and skill as evidenced particularly in his innings at Old Trafford and his 86 at Bombay against the West Indies which was punctuated with brilliant strokes against the pace of Roberts. His aggregate read 1467, an average of 48.9 and a full career ahead. He was clearly learning through actual experience, of the intricacies and complexities of the game in all its varied aspects. With an alert mind and a sensibility to respond to the flux of life and the game, an awakening to its realities would inevitably mould, shape and develop his character. It was now left to him to examine the discordant threads and impose on his career a sense of discipline and coherence in order to soar to greater heights.

CHAPTER 4

The Years Of Burgeoning

In the pomp of proud audacious deeds.

Christopher Marlowe: Tamburlaine

The infinite variety of life with its complexities, apprehensions, pain, anguish, thrill, joy, excitement is experienced in varying degrees of intensity in the course of one's life. To the casual and indifferent the challenges are routine and insignificant, but to the sensitive and idealistic or the ambitious the challenges are demanding, the vicissitudes intolerable, the pleasures profound. To emerge beyond the mire and complexity requires strength of character and resilience. To the sensitive Sunil, conscious of the audience's expectations, the demands were growing. Fully cognizant of them, he knew that meeting the challenge consistently was herculean.

Hampered by his finger injury and lack of peak cricketing form, though he had scored a resounding 86 in the last Test against the West Indies, he tried feverishly to regain consistent form with an opportunity in the Ranji Trophy matches. A century in the second consecutive year eluded him and this was disturbing, especially with the approaching 1975-76 season.... a visit to New Zealand followed by an expedition to the Caribbean.

But before this, India were scheduled for a World Cup appearance in January 1975. Prior to their departure, the cricketers were requested to assemble at Wankhede Stadium in Bombay for a one week practice session. Since Sunil was a 'local' player he was allowed by his manager to spend his nights at home. During their stay, the President of the Cricket Control Boardwas critical of him for not conforming to the

Board's policy, especially as he was the vice-captain deputizing for the captain Venkataraghavan who was performing duties in England. It was felt that Sunil's presence and the presence of everyone at all times would develop team spirit. This Sunil found laughable and this was indicative of the insolence of office which cricketers at times experienced. On Sunil's part he could have defended himself since he was given permission by the manager G.S. Ramchand. But when Solkar was confronted with the same question, he deceived the President into believing that he was staying at the Stadium. Sunil was disturbed by the manager's failure to accept responsibility for allowing both himself and Solkar to overnight at home. He was also disappointed by Solkar's response for he was well within his rights as he had got permission to stay at home. He could not understand why a Test cricketer particularly one of the calibre of Eknath Solkar should be afraid of a mere cricket administrator. Solkar clearly revealed a failure of strength of character and this disturbed and hurt Sunil.

Sunil's reaction was an indication of his readiness to assert himself once convinced of the merits or strength of his conviction or his conduct. Though to many he seemed self-effacing, it did not signify that he would not heroically champion the cause and welfare of contemporary cricketers during his career.

India were now thrust into one-day cricket with the Prudential Cup ahead and the players were pitted against one-day specialists and this did not portend any good for them. For Sunil the series held its critical torment. His first one-day appearance against England can be described as one of the enigmas of his career performances, seemingly beyond the intelligible. In retrospect, it can be deemed a rare moment of aberration or a dissociation of sensibility, of not responding to the forces and demands of the game. To him it was a "complete mental block".

In the match, England in a spectacular fashion accumulated quite a towering total of 334 in 60 overs. In response Sunil did not seem to address the task with the approach it deserved.

He had stayed at the crease for the full duration of the innings and scored a paltry 36, a negative and unforgivable batting display. It was disappointing to his team mates; it invited howls of protest from the crowd and this intensified his discomfiture; it was disconcerting and disheartening for him. In an expression of his dilemma at the crease he recalls that "by far, it was the worst innings I have ever played. There were occasions when I felt like moving away from the stumps, so that I would be bowled. This was the only way to get away from the mental agony from which I was suffering. I was dropped thrice, off fairly easy chances too. I was in a curious position. I couldn't force the pace and I couldn't get out, even when I tried to. Towards the end I was playing mechanically."

At the wicket he actually envisaged no possibility of escape; his training and discipline had forsaken him and he seemed imprisoned in his anxiety and reduced to weary drudgery. His state of mind echoes the poet John Donne's line "Tis all in pieces, all coherence gone" reflecting both intellectual contemplation and mental agony.

Ted Dexter, a former England captain, coach and manager who admired Sunil as a master craftsman, was disappointed in this display. In commenting he said:
"There was no sense, rhythm or reason in his performance. He should have been pulled off the field by his captain. Nothing less than a vote of censure by the International Cricket Council would satisfy me if I had paid good money through the turnstiles only to be shortchanged by a display such as Gavaskar's."

On his return home he was summoned by the Board to explain the nature of his performance and was shocked to learn of the manager's report that he persisted in playing dull cricket and its demoralizing effect on the young players. To compound his predicament he was also accused of an 'aloofness', a detachment from the players. By this criticism he was not enthused. Though the enquiry was dropped, it meant that the Board members had censured him critically and would have had reservations about him. To him it was an illustration of the human insensitivity which he often faced during his career.

The predicament he faced during the Prudential Cup series, the knowledge that he did not fully enjoy the 1974 West Indian series in India through injury and the inconsistency of form at first class cricket were dispiriting to him and in a positive mood tried to recapture in his cricket a new spirit, a vitality and energy that would eclipse any gloom that lingered. In a mood of dejection he said: "I was feeling downcast and was disinterested in almost everything." With determination he assumed the captaincy of Bombay and was intent on bringing glory to that prestigious position and to his personal batting performance. During this period he was approached to make an appearance in a Marathi film "Premachi Salvi" which he eventually did; before this he had the experience of appearing in commercials but this was an interesting diversion and a novel experience for him.

Magnificent batting displays which earned him three consecutive centuries in the Ranji Trophy competition and a double century against Sri Lanka in an unofficial Test were reasons to brighten his spirits and enhance his personal prospects for the approaching tours to New Zealand and the West Indies.

The rigours of touring began with a visit to New Zealand early in 1976. Early during the tour Bedi was suffering from a muscular problem and Sunil as deputy was given the opportunity to lead India for the first time. This he made use of and though he thought that he struggled to make a century, the sixth in his career, he set a good example for his team. India eventually won by eight wickets despite the dubious umpiring decisions which plagued the tour. With great joy and delight Sunil uttered: "It was exhilarating to win my first Test as captain."

Bedi was back at the helm for the second and third Tests. The second ended in a draw and the third saw India comprehensively beaten. But the sensitive Sunil was disillusioned by umpiring decisions; he felt there was a concerted effort to ensure that New Zealand did not lose the series even if they did not emerge victorious. Media coverage also revealed the unabashed partiality of the New Zealand press. Though Sunil performed creditably he was unfortunate during the last Test to be struck by a ball while fielding. It resulted in a broken jaw bone.

There is the perennial issue or problem concerning umpiring decisions and reports of incompetence or bold criticism of umpires' honesty or fair play. It is not strange to read reports of umpiring decisions after touring teams complete their missions abroad. The sporting headlines usually make capital of this issue. In Sunil's case, as a player wounded by decisions affecting his and his team's performance, he articulated his complaints in his "Sunny Days". But not only did Sunil give vent to his criticism, but later according to Marshneil, David Gower (perhaps unnerved by Sunil's attack on English umpiring) did mention in a cricket book that it was impossible to have Gavaskar out LBW in India. To this, Marshneil in stout defence, responded by emphasizing that in the approximately 170 innings in Test cricket he was given out LBW more times in India than abroad. It is interesting to hear Gower's response to this but her assertion and her response to Gower's statement echoes T.S.Eliot's "wholly insignificant grouse."

On this subject of umpiring, there are other issues to be taken into consideration by cricketing boards which may help towards achieving less confrontation between players and umpires. For example, recruitment procedures in selecting umpires should be more rigid in terms of one's physical fitness, eyesight, hearing, skill, knowledge of the game and strength of character. His resilience and scrupulous integrity are most essential if he is to stand firmly amidst the crowd's impetuosity, partisan nature and volatile behaviour and even at times players' irrational tantrums on the field. This may seem very demanding but in the light of the fierce competitive nature of the modern game, the arbiters must be equipped to assert the mantle of infallibility and mature judgement.

The vexed question of neutral umpires has been one which has exercised the minds of administrators, players and the cricket public with increased fervour within recent years. Advocates of the advantages to be derived from having them are convinced that such a scheme will go a long way to diffuse Test match rows and controversy over controversial umpiring decisions, which have tended to mar so many modern Test series, creating acrimony between opposing players.

To assist the arbiters of the game, the I.C.C. has enlisted the aid of modern technology and the camera; the third umpire (in the pavilion) is called in to adjudicate in close cases involving run-outs, stumpings, and some disputed catches, (though strangely enough, not LBWs). Television replays in slow motion are clearly a big help - yet one feels that angles can be deceptive and the camera can lie on occasion. Even so, there are times when television replays can prove embarrassing to an umpire who may rule in favour of a batsman for a run out appeal and seconds later, the camera shows he was still inches out of his crease when the wicket was broken; or vice versa. The pressures are intense for all.

Though most cricketers, whatever their reservations and misgivings, do abide by umpiring decisions, the question arises: Should they meekly take the rough with the smooth and eschew all semblance of dissent (as the code of conduct requires them to do now) or should they perhaps be given the opportunity to point out rationally those apparent flaws in umpiring decisions which seem obvious? How this should be done is clearly a matter for the I.C.C. to decide.

Over the last two decades, forceful and rebellious personalities like Ian Chappell, Dennis Lillee, John Snow, Viv Richards, Ian Botham and also Sunil Gavaskar himself have expressed strong disapproval over decisions.

Though Sunil Gavaskar on several occasions expressed dissatisfaction with umpiring decisions he was very well aware of the demands made on umpires. He advocated, together with his contemporaries Allan Lamb, Desmond Haynes, Malcolm Marshall, Ian Chappell for the use of neutral umpires towards solution of the problem:

"Today, although most Test umpires do a good job, it is obvious that they sometimes feel under pressure from the home crowd. Where neutral umpires have been used they have been a resounding success. Even when an error occurs, and is confirmed by television playback, people realise that it is a genuine mistake and not a question of bias."

Though there has been some progress with the use of the neutral umpires and the third umpire with the advantage of the camera, it relates only to certain decisions.

It is recommended here that not all close incidents be referred to the camera; but, what happens in very rare and unusual instances as that catching incident witnessed at Kensington in Barbados in March 1995 when Brian Lara was adjudged caught by the Australian fieldsman, Steve Waugh? It might have been worthwhile for the umpire to look at the camera as most viewers were clearly in doubt. But then, do the existing laws of the game make provision for that?

The West Indian tour was next on the agenda, but Sunil was incapacitated once more. On his first tour to the Caribbean it was a finger injury, now a fractured jaw needed time for recovery. It meant his absence from the early matches in the Caribbean, but he was back, though he experienced some measure of unease and apprehension before resuming play. The only measure of consolation was his happy memories of the 1971 tour and with confidence he approached the series. The first Test at Barbados was disastrous. A meagre 177 in India's first innings was rebuffed by a brisk 488. A second innings total of 214 was abysmal and India suffered an embarrassing defeat.

Sunil started his first innings on a positive note; he cut, drove and hooked Roberts and Holding but during his aggressive strokeplay, a shooter from Roberts trapped him LBW. He failed in the second innings and the hope to restore his Caribbean image would be in Trinidad for the second Test. The West Indies had won handsomely in Barbados and it was left to India to demonstrate its courage after its early loss.

The second Test in Trinidad proved to be a thriller but India failed to grasp victory. Deceived by a strong spin attack West Indies managed a slender 241 with only Richards, with a belligerent century and to a lesser extent Murray, offering any form of resistance.

India's response here would certainly have determined the outcome of the match. Gavaskar in heroic fashion seemed determined to control and dictate events on the field. He simply had to compensate for his atrocious batting during the second innings at Kensington Oval and this he did. Ravi Chaturvedi, Indian sportswriter and commentator, describes his tenure at the crease as "confidence incarnate." He offered a straight bat to the balls on the stump and ignored the bouncers. It was an innings of craftsmanship, of application to the task and superb punishment of loose balls with grace and power. With Brijesh Patel, he continued to score freely, stroking Holding handsomely and aggressively. A majestic straight drive and an elegant cover drive signalled to Roberts his intentions. The partnership grew in confidence with Patel becoming more enterprising and eventually India, at 402 for five, declared. It was Sunil's seventh Test century with a score of 156 and it was his second in two months. In the second innings the West Indians offered no great resistance to the Indian spin attack and when stumps were drawn with West Indians at 215 for 8, the Indians could have asserted openly that they were in the ascendancy in this Test match. This encounter brought life to the series and aroused spectator interest during the rest of the series.

Guyana was the venue for the third Test but rainy weather posed a threat to the match. In order to avoid abandonment of play, the match was rescheduled for Trinidad. In the interim, before returning to Trinidad the Indian team did enjoy its stay. One special event of note was a trick played on the manager Polly Umrigar and treasurer Balu Alagnan on April 1, All Fool's Day. A phone call was arranged by Bedi and made to Umrigar requesting that he report to the Indian High Commissioner in Guyana to account for the Indian team's bad behaviour during the second Test in Trinidad. Umrigar, in great uneasiness, rushed to Bedi's room to inform him of the telephone call. Umrigar in his anxiety said he did not even have Guyanese currency for the taxi fare. Bedi then advised him to go and find out the truth of the matter. To make the circumstances less mitigating, Umrigar took a letter from the New Zealand Cricket Council which had praised the Indian team's behaviour. It was on the way to the Indian High Commissioner's office that Balu realized it could be an April Fool's joke and that Sunil was capable of stage-managing such a joke and he felt that Sunil should have gone along with them. Umrigar in haste wanted to attend to the matter quickly so they speedily went along only to discover it was a trick played on them. Both Polly and Balu however very sportingly took the joke in good stride.

These long tours were usually fraught with problems of food, travel, hotel accommodation, adverse weather conditions, injuries, tensions of the game; but Sunil would always recall the happy times in the presence of Solkar, Engineer, Mankad. These, through their antics and humour would lighten the tension. There were often other diversions which added some flavour to the tours. Sunil relates an incident where he was accosted by a Guyanese girl who made a proposal of marriage to him. It turned out that the girl was interested in acting in India and she saw him as the means of entry into India. If he had married her then her problems would have been solved.

Sunil's fan club of 1971 in the Caribbean, especially in Trinidad, did include among the passionate lovers of cricket, a large contingent of the feminine gender. It was a thrill to stand in the ladies members' stand at the Queen's Park Oval after the end of the day's play and observe the multitude of young girls in their multi-coloured finery, with autograph books, handkerchiefs, paper, T-shirts, or miniature bats crowding around and trying to attract his attention in the players pavilion; many of them used the autograph as a ruse to be familiar with him. It seemed that the separation of the cricketers' area, part of the Queen's Park Club pavilion, from the rest of the spectators was the escape route for Sunil. Here females and non members are denied entry or access. Had it not been so, Sunil may have been tempted to go the way of Subash Gupte or Dicky Rutnagur and we may never have heard of Marshneil. That would indeed have been a great loss to us all but more especially to Sunil.

Very often he was in the middle of practical jokes and was very popular for his imitations of individual cricketers with whom he was familiar. For this reason he showed displeasure whenever he was accused of being aloof and detached from his fellow players. He had strongly defended himself on this allegation and noted that only during his captaincy periods when he was allotted a single room that there were periods when he confined himself to plan strategies and concentrate on the game.

From Guyana the players returned to the Queen's Park Oval for their third encounter. This proved to be an historic one for the Indians won this Test in a rare victory in cricket history. India was set the task of scoring 402 runs to win (Lloyd had declared at 271 for 6). This challenge India met bravely and amassed 406 runs for the loss of 4 wickets. It was only the second time this feat was achieved; the first time being in 1948 by Bradman's team over an English team at Leeds in England in very much the same fashion. However, in 1979 India very nearly achieved this feat against England when they were set a total of 438 for victory. Spearheaded by Sunil with 221 runs the Indians rose to the challenge just narrowly missing victory.

However, this Test victory at the Queen's Park Oval was the

result of great team effort. It was the application of Amarnath and the centuries by both Gavaskar and Vishwanath, together with the successes of the spinners in both innings that were responsible for their victory. This match marked Sunil's 8th Test century and when he was on 47 he achieved his 2000th run in Test cricket in his 23rd Test appearance. He was clearly blossoming and enjoying his successes.

However, after all the jubilation and triumphant excesses which followed victory, Sabina's final Test was an event, unsavoury and bitter. It was a match which would appear ugly and evil in the memory, a stain on cricket's image. The West Indians, prior to this series with India, had been severely battered at the hands of Thomson and Lillee with their terrifying pace. They had suffered a humiliating 5-1 defeat. This offensive by the Australians was infectious as the West Indians had learnt that aggression was the solution to supremacy. In the series against India, the Indians, after their first Test defeat, were playing positive cricket. At no stage after the first Test could the West Indies assert their superiority or claim ascendancy in the series. But events suggested that Lloyd, with a diminished stature, was bent on capturing the series, even if it meant employing bitter and ugly methods.

Simon Wilde in "Letting Rip", an interesting narrative of the catalogue of atrocities and cruelty meted out to batsmen by ferocious and intimidatory bowling, goes the full length to describe the debacle which has been labelled the "Battle of Kingston". In his explicit commentary of this debacle, Wilde claims that the killer instinct was shown from the start. This extract taken from "Letting Rip" illustrates the intensity and austerity of the incident:

"The killer instinct was on show from the start. On a pitch offering bounce but little real pace, Lloyd's fast bowlers, Holding, Daniel and Holder, persistently dug the ball in short. To make matters worse, the pitch had recently been relaid and there was a ridge at one end which made the bounce there vary alarmingly. Holding repeatedly bowled bouncers and even

1st Test England v India at the Old Trafford 1974.

4th Test England v India, Oval 1979.

*Sunil Gavaskar in action. Wasim Bari, Safraz Nawaz and Javed Miandad.
2nd Test Pakistan v India, Lahore, 1978.*

Prudential World Cup India v West Indies Lord's, 1983.

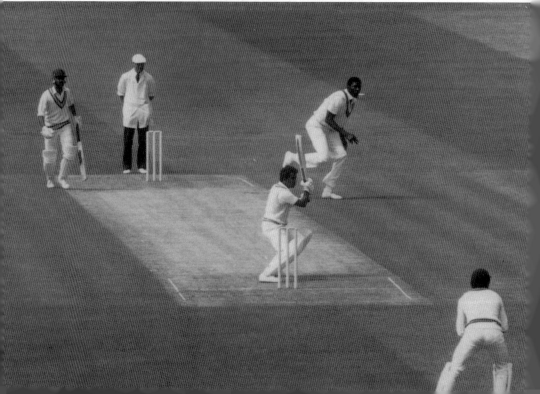

Here Ian Botham signs the plaster-cast on Sunil's leg. His leg was broken fielding at silly-point while Botham was batting. 3rd Test England v India at the Oval, 1982.

1971. West Indies v India. The joys of cricket. Bernard Julien, Roodal Mahelal, 1 ardent fan) Ajit Wadekar, Gary Sobers and Sunil among the crowd at the end of the series, (Queen's Prak Oval).

Azhar, Sunil and Sachin or Present and Past with Future?
Sunil at a dinner party listens to Imran Khan.

resorted to going round the wicket. Several times the batsmen were struck on the body and fingers. Nevertheless, India, having been put in by Lloyd and shown great courage, finished the first day on 178 for one.

Then a remarkable thing happened. During the night, a noticeable layer of grass sprouted on the pitch. It is hardly an exaggeration to say that this unusual sprouting changed the course of cricket history. Here were the green shoots of recovery that Lloyd had been looking for. "It was immediately obvious that (the pitch) was going to be faster and more dangerous," said Tony Cozier. Batting was an even more daunting proposition than it had been the day before. Vishwanath had a finger both fractured and dislocated as he was caught off the glove to a ball from Holding; Patel, who had never looked at ease against pace even when making runs, took his eyes off a ball from Holder and edged it into his mouth and Gaekwad, after having survived seven and a half hours, was struck above the left ear by a delivery whose bounce bore no relation to its length. There were several other terrifying deliveries, including one to Viswanath which, according to Sunil Gavaskar, "almost took his head with it." With six wickets down, Bishen Bedi, the India captain, did what no other captain has had the temerity to do (although many in their time must have longed to do so) by declaring the innings closed in order to protect himself - and Chandrasekhar - from the risk of being hurt. ("It's not that I'm afraid to die. I just don't want to be there when it happens..."). Wilde further claims that Lloyd's reaction revealed that he was not upset by the incident.

"If you can't play quick bowling, you shouldn't be in the game at international level," he said. In addition to this Holding declared it was war at Kingston and Richards in a calmer disposition stated that the Indians had "over-dramatized the dangers."

This incident, it was felt, dramatized the predicament of Lloyd as a man in defeat; his was a reaction to the pressures of captaincy after the defeat by Australia and the quite formidable opposition by the Indians. The game which embodies the distinguishing ancestral virtues of sportsmanship, courage, heroism now seemed to have lost its idealism; it was a dissolution of a school of cricket that promoted the game as a gentleman's game and this form of intimidation was against the conventional norms of the game; a victory here was therefore not considered heroic or splendid but hollow and debased.

Sunil was moved to the point where he complained to umpire Gosein about the intimidatory nature of the bowling. He was also disgusted by the crowd's behaviour, their insensitivity and callousness. He was the only member of the team to resist courageously the lethal onslaught with 66 to his credit. It is interesting to note that while on one or two occasions he complained of intimidatory bowling, he never showed fear openly. He expressed respect for some extremely fast spells he encountered but never caved in; he always fought the battle. Simon Wilde's statistical record of injuries to batsmen between 1974-1994 reveals that it was only on one occasion that Gavaskar was hit whilst facing fast bowling.

The series concluded with a victory to the West Indies. The results at Sabina gave them the lead but it must be said that cricket's image was tarnished. Though the tour ended on a bitter note there was much to make Sunil happy. His son was born while he was in New Zealand and he would now be seeing him for the first time on his return to India. Based on his admiration and respect for the remarkable batting star Rohan Kanhai, Sunil named his son Rohan. Also at the end of the full tour he had added three centuries and scored 656 runs in seven Test marches. Later in the year there would be two touring teams visiting India; New Zealand's tour would be followed by England and it was expected that within the calendar year he would have acquired 1000 runs, another milestone for the record books.

The demands of Test cricket had increased since early 1976. The tour to New Zealand was followed by the tour to the

West Indies. This tour, though a personal success for Sunil, was sullied by the "growing murderousness" of Test cricket. It was as if "the blood-dimmed tide was loosed and the ceremony of innocence drowned." The effect on Sunil was recorded vividly in his "Sunny Days". His fearlessness and courage in making known his views was characteristic of him. Some, even in India, thought him arrogant and aloof. For this outspoken, candid assertion of his beliefs, he came into conflict with many who tried to detract from his performance. It must not be construed that he deliberately wielded an axe but when inflamed by the oppressors wrong he was courageous.

In this particular year, Sunil's summer harvest of runs excited the populace. To attain 1000 runs in Test cricket in one calendar year would be historic, not only for India, but as a remarkable feat on the international scene. And India waited on him to display his talent at home; his successes so far were greater on foreign soil.

His first Test against New Zealand at his home ground in Bombay was a great delight. He scored his first Test century of 119 at home and in the process chalked up his fourth century of 1976. The second Test also yielded reasonable scores and brought him nearer the 1000 runs mark with his personal aggregate being 870; but after the third Test he was still short of the milestone. Needless to say his contribution to his team's effort was considerable in helping India to a 2-1 victory over New Zealand. Though expectation for the 1000 mark was high he did not attain it in this series; he was still 85 runs short of the target but with one more Test within the calendar year of 1976. The crowd's expectancy brought a fair measure of pressure on the batsman. He declared: "With almost everybody willing me to score 1000 in the year, the pressure was intense." His priority, he maintained, was to give the innings a solid foundation.

In the last Test played in 1976 (which was the first Test in the series against England) Sunil achieved the 1000 run mark reaching 1024 in the calendar year. And he did it splendidly against the spin of Underwood with a score of 71 although India was defeated in that Test. He became the first Indian player to score 1000 runs in a calendar year and in the process was thickening the files of his statistical record.

After the fulfilment of a fertile and productive 1976, there was a period of drought for Sunil and India. England rode roughshod over them in their first three matches with resounding wins at Delhi, Calcutta and Madras. Sunil was experiencing a bad trot with five innings of 0, 18, 39, 24 and 4. It was only during the second innings of the fourth Test that he seemed a shadow of the hero of 1976. With Vishwanath he helped India redeem themselves somewhat and also lifted their morale a bit during the series. With sheer technical skill he used footwork against the well-flighted ball and demonstrated to Underwood the nature of his skill. His innings of a half-century was described by Wisden as one of "great technical skill". It was said that the wicket was like a minefield and that he could have batted on a corrugated roof. Both he and Vishwanath, with typical confident style and sureness of touch, saw India reverse their fortunes with India eventually winning that match by 140 runs. It was becoming more and more apparent that if these two did not perform, India would be at the mercy of their opponents. Sunil felt strongly that ability and talent were not India's problems; but rather that the players were not developing or exploiting their potential. Could it be lack of commitment or enthusiasm?

The final encounter with England brought him his tenth Test century; it was quite an outstanding feat to achieve this in his 32nd Test and it meant that he was scoring, on an average, one century in almost every 3 Tests. In this particular match which ended in a draw and saw England clinch a 3-1 margin of victory, Sunil was at the centre of yet another controversy. In this match he was given the role of opening bowler, a rare but occasionally much-needed role. The English opener, Dennis Amiss alleged that he was deliberately following through on the pitch in an attempt to create a spot on the wicket to be

later exploited by the spinners. The conflict escalated to the extent that the umpires were called upon to intervene. The cynics did of course refer to his petulance and fiery temperament. Sunil, however, explained that he knew Dennis as one of the nicest cricketers and felt that the tension of the series and the pressures of playing in India accounted for his behaviour. "The only ball I followed through on the wicket" he said, "was the one I bowled from near the stumps for which I was slightly warned; but it certainly wasn't deliberate. One could hardly create a spot in one or two overs."
Bob Willis remarked:
"Only once has Sunil annoyed me and that was when he opened the bowling and blatantly followed through to sear the wicket for the spinners."

Manohar S.Kamath, in the 'Onlooker' published an article entitled "Gavaskar: No more a Gentleman Cricketer" in which he criticized Gavaskar's tantrums on the cricket field and cited a number of incidents. In communicative urgency, he responded, expressing his objection to Kamath's deliberate attempt to malign him. He felt it amounted to defamation. He countered all the incidents raised by Kamath and of this one with Amiss he remarked that it was Amiss' duty to inform the umpire of his wrong doing. "Since he chose to shout at me, I had to talk back," was Sunil's explanation. Sunil was aggrieved by this criticism and felt such adverse comments could harm his career and reputation in the cricket world. On a very serious note he requested the magazine's editors to offer a public expression of regret for the harm caused.

The series which had been depressing for India after the third Test, brightened slightly with an Indian victory in the fourth Test and a draw in the final encounter. There was constant evaluation of Gavaskar's performance against England and it was felt that his two centuries and a few fifties were no indication that he had fully mastered the English bowling, especially when comparisons were made with his performance against the West Indies and New Zealand attack. The critics, however, thought that he had the benefit of youth and there was a great amount of cricket to be played in the future. One of the more demanding challenges to his craft would be seen during the Australian tour in 1977. And at this stage, his successes at first class level at home both in the Ranji and Duleep competitions brought to him a spirit of optimism. This sense of confidence he needed as a fitting prelude to the Australian Test encounter.

The five Test Australia-India series concluded with the records showing a 3-2 lead in favour of Australia; but beyond the statistics it is interesting to know the details of the story. In the first Test Indian players had only themselves to blame for their loss; for at different stages of the game they failed to grasp the initiative to establish their supremacy and in the end were beaten by a margin of 16 runs. Gavaskar's contribution was 3 and 113; he had added another century to his career. This he followed by scoring two more consecutive centuries in the second and third Tests. India were, however, defeated again in the second Test by a narrow margin of two wickets in a high scoring match. Melbourne saw him acquiring his third century in the series and in the process a courageous India demonstrated its latent fighting spirit with a resounding 222 run victory. Victory was made possible by Gavaskar's contribution both in the field and on the batting pitch but more so by Chandrasekhar's match winning figures of 12 for 104. This victory was an historic one for India for it was their first on Australian grounds.

The fourth Test followed at Sydney and India equalled the series by an overwhelming victory of one innings. At this point they were 2-2. In the final contest both sides stroked their way profusely and it was only 47 runs which separated Australia from India at the conclusion with Australia emerging the victors. The records reveal that Gavaskar failed in this final encounter and though India lost, it was by a narrow margin. The batsmen performed with pride in combating the Australian challenge. (In fairness it should be stated that

Australia were without their Packer-contracted stars: the Chappell brothers, Doug Walters and Lillee). Bobby Simpson was 'resurrected' to lead the team.

The events of the series emphasized the fact that India's potential if fully exploited could reap richer rewards and instill greater confidence in their skill and ability. Batsmen showed that they were capable of coming to terms with the pace of Thomson and Clark and this was certainly an achievement and a morale booster for India in their future encounters. For Gavaskar, his thirteenth Test century signalled a new Indian record; he had surpassed Polly Umrigar's twelve centuries, the highest held previously by an Indian batsman. He was also within striking distance of Umrigar's record Test aggregate of 3631 runs. In the latter years of the seventies as his craft flourished and burgeoned, new records were established for the younger generation to challenge in the interest of Indian cricket.

The 1978 series against Pakistan was part of a packed agenda for India. A visit by the West Indies would follow at the end of 1978 and India would then travel to England in mid 1979. The encounter with Pakistan proved to be historic for Gavaskar. It had been eighteen years since the last encounter between these two countries, India and Pakistan. Because of political problems in the sixties there existed between them an uneasy and strained relationship. Sporting relationships, as a result, suffered and Test cricket was discontinued. There has been a history of tension since the sub-continent of India was divided in 1947 to form the mainly Muslim state of Pakistan and India retaining the majority of Hindus in its populace. Right up to 1960 their encounters were always tension-packed and rivalry was always fierce and frightening. With an apparent calm the series began, and with it, underlying tension. In reply to Pakistan's first innings score of 503 for 8 declared, Gavaskar and Chetan Chauhan were treated to hostile, intimidatory bowling by Safraz Nawaz. During this confrontation Gavaskar called for his captain. It was reported by the press that here Gavaskar was reacting against Nawaz' hostility. But in fact the incident, according to C.D.Clark in his book 'The Record-breaking Gavaskar', was of a different nature. Gavaskar had realized that the umpires watches were not synchronized. There was a difference of twenty minutes between the watches and there was no clock at the ground. Gavaskar remarked that he had to establish the true time for it was always crucial in a game. In response to the much circulated news of his reacting to the hostility of Nawaz he recalls:

"I don't think Chetan and I were bothered by bumpers because we thought it was a waste of a new ball."

His score of 89 clearly showed that the bouncers were insignificant. India's response was a strong 462 for 9 and this high scoring on both sides ensured a drawn match.

On the last morning of play another incident occurred and again Gavaskar was in the middle of it all. It was alleged that he had made an unfavourable remark about the umpire. This was not well received and a protest was lodged next morning. However, a superficial reconciliation in the form of a handshake was arrived at before play began.

The second Test at Lahore began with Pakistan emerging victorious. In a bid to save the match with a draw, Gavaskar's and Chauhan's brave attempts were met with controversial decisions. Chauhan was given out first and the manner of Gavaskar's departure at 97 angered him. He made his feelings clear as he proceeded to the pavilion:

"I was annoyed because we were making a terrific fightback. First Chetan was the victim of a bad decision and then it was me."

Though India's spirit of combat was enterprising, Pakistan won; it was the first time after 14 attempts that a decisive conclusion to a game had been reached.

The climate of tension seemed to demoralize the Indians' spirit and the final Test at Karachi went to Pakistan with an eight wicket victory. The only bright flicker on India's side was the sterling performance of Gavaskar who scored a century in each innings of this Test. It was of great historic significance because it was the second time he had achieved this feat. In 1971 during his debut tour to the Caribbean he had done the same. He was now among a select list of five players to have achieved this distinction. The record of scoring a century against each Test playing country was another of his achievements at Karachi; but he was not singular in this respect for Vishwanath had also accomplished this feat. The records also revealed that he had overtaken Polly Umrigar's Test aggregate, the highest by an Indian before Gavaskar's effort here.

Gavaskar's display was a continuation of a fulfiling period in his career. There was daring, determination, concentration, acute mental aptitude, all qualities or factors which contributed to his admirable performances; achievement was informed not only by physical dexterity but an intellectual grasp of the various and complex opposing forces he engaged with. He was always the cynosure of all eyes; in his team he was the lynchpin and the force who had to inspire by example; and to the opposition he was the chief target. His role was exceptionally different from the others and its demands were intense and critical; his image had to be preserved through his performances and personal supportive presence in the team.

The India-Pakistan series was a personal success for Gavaskar but it meant the demise of skipper Bedi. The Board retained the services of Bedi as a player but elected Gavaskar to the post of captain, an additional responsibility.

The West Indies-India series followed and Gavaskar assumed the leadership role. The picture at a glance reveals that India won the six test series 1-0. Gavaskar's continuing monopoly, his enhanced and irrepressible dynamic performances at the crease ensured India's ascendancy though critics felt that the killer instinct in Gavaskar was missing; it was thought in some circles that India would have won more handsomely had the captain been more enterprising. But to many others, Gavaskar had demonstrated that he could cope with the burden of captaincy and also perform successfully in his original and major role as a batsman.

The West Indies, though not the victors, performed very creditably without the resources of their best players who were engaged in the Packer assignment in Australia. But they started on a positive note and did well particularly during the first half of the series. After this, their inexperience and the hardship of a long tour seemed to affect their performance. There were commendable performances from Faoud Bacchus, both on the field and at the crease; Kallicharan excelled at his batting, and Shivnarine, Clarke, Holder and Marshall all showed their mettle.

The first Test was filled with high scores. Gavaskar in a prolific mood scored 205 and 73. In his own inimitable style he followed up with a dismissal off the first ball of the second Test, only to deceive for a short period. He was back in an aggressive mood in the third Test with centuries of 107 and 182 not out. With this almost theatrical dramatization of his superior skills and plundering mood he became the only batsman in Test cricket to score a century in each innings on three occasions. In the process another Indian Test record was established when both he and Vengsarkar shared an unbroken 344 second wicket partnership. This performance of Gavaskar's would register in the statistical records that in 78 days he had accomplished the marvelous and stupendous feat of scoring 1014 runs. The period encompassed here was between 16th October 1978 to the 2nd January 1979. This feat of scoring 1000 runs was achieved by England's Wally Hammond in the 1930's but done in 124 days. Another look at the records will show that in his performance at Calcutta in the third Test he had equalled Ken Barrington's record of the only batsman to score 1000 runs in a calendar year on two occasions.

Though he failed at Madras in the fourth Test he engineered India's sole victory of the series. In typical fashion he returned to the crease in the fifth Test and recorded another century of 120. He was in a belligerent mood with an insatiable appetite during the sixth and final Test but he only scored 40 out of a total of 644 runs. This included 18 in one over from Marshall.

The series was successful for India. The incomparable display of batsmanship during the Australian, Pakistani and West Indian series indicated his world class status and his artistry. Superlative descriptions of his successes may sound trite and commonplace if repeated here. Some critics thought it prudent to await India's 1979 series to reassess his craftsmanship if they were to accord him the prestigious accolade as the finest opening batsman not only of contemporary cricket but one of the finest of all times.

Kerry Packer's brand of cricket had attracted the great cricketing talents throughout the cricketing world with the exception of India. But the desire to play among the greats and the attractive financial package Packer presented to the players were tempting to Gavaskar. He indicated a desire to join Packer but on condition that he would revert to his country once it needed his cricketing services. Players who were approached by Packer in India needed that assurance from Packer and were willing to negotiate with the Indian Cricket Board on those grounds. This move angered the Board and as a result Gavaskar was not selected captain for the Indian tour of England in mid 1979. It so happened that before the series began Packer and the International Cricket Council settled their dispute. But to England Gavaskar went as player; the Board had appointed Venkataraghavan as captain and Vishwanath as his deputy.

The Prudential World Cup competition prefaced the Test series between England and India and it gave critics justification to consign India to mediocrity. Their performance was pathetic in all three matches, even against Sri Lanka, a team which did not even enjoy Test status at that time. This display gave the English critics ammunition to demoralize India's credibility as a Test team. They were critical of the batting strength and indicated that only Gavaskar and Vishwanath were not suspect against English conditions. But before the Test series India showed signs of brilliance in the matches preceding the Tests and this enhanced their spirit and confidence. What was unnerving at this time and some thought it deliberate, was the vicious campaign by the press to undermine the Indian medium pacer, Karsan Ghavri. It was publicized that his bowling was suspect and that his action was illegal. During the MCC match at Lord's, Ghavri had struck Brearley and Larkins and in the process had taken a number of wickets.

The first Test concluded with defeat for India. It was done handsomely but it must be mentioned that India's attack was depleted through injury and fitness problems. This augured well for English batting. In response to England's 633 for 5 declared, India was bowled out for a paltry 207. Gavaskar's contribution was a confident 61 before he was unluckily run out. This he followed up with a neat 68 in the second innings. With only Gavaskar and Vishwanath batting with assurance, India succumbed to a disastrous defeat.

Before the second Test started, Gavaskar recorded a century against Gloucestershire and this brought him to another milestone in his career. It was his 50th first class century and had he played more first class cricket in England his statistical figures would have certainly been very different. In that second Test, India scored a paltry and undistinguished 96 runs; a demoralizing blow to their spirit. Of this total, Gavaskar managed 42 and Vishwanath 21 in their combative strike. It was an England's lead of 323 that stared India in the face as the second innings began. Gavaskar went for 59 and it was Vishwanath together with Vengsarkar who firmly resisted the English attack with centuries to their credit. They defied the English desperate attempt to clinch victory. The outcome was sobering; India's performance was deserving of respect.

India's batting began to show promise but in the third Test because of rain there was nothing significant except for Botham's brilliant Test century and Gavaskar's effort which was short of a century by 22 runs. He was showing a great consistency but not the big imposing scores to set the English scribes afire. He would at this time, have been experiencing moments of tension and anxiety for the tour was approaching its final stages and there was no outstanding performance to cherish.

At the end of the first innings of the final Test England had accumulated 305 and reduced India's score to 202. It was a lead of 103. After the completion of England's second innings, India was invited to score 437 runs, an imposing and formidable task.

India's morale, reputation and batting strength were now going to be truly tested. Did the players possess the moral fibre, courage and skill to assert themselves and prove worthy of Test class? In response Sunil Gavaskar and Chetan Chauhan emerged heroic. From the fourth day into the fifth day before the partnership came to an end at 213, India's mettle was significantly shown. Nor did Vengsarkar withdraw from the adversaries. He and Sunil bravely continued and established a partnership worth 153. India's hope of victory looked optimistic but at 429 for 8 play ended, 8 runs short of the target with two wickets in hand. Sunil had been dismissed for 221 and therefore was not there at the end to make a final bid for victory.

However, it was Sunil's brilliant double century which was the focus of attention. The records of Indian cricket had to be re-written. He had passed Vinoo Mankad's 184 against England; now his was the highest by an Indian player against England both at home and abroad. Previously, Pataudi Jnr had scored 203 in the 1963-64 series. Sunil was the first Indian player to score three double hundreds.

It was significant that Sunil performed and excelled in his last innings against England on this tour. It was a fitting close to a season and it convincingly dispelled the doubts of the English who were reluctant to laud him as he deserved. Those who witnessed his flawless display of craft, extolled his virtues with great sincerity. One of the game's true batting geniuses,

Sir Len Hutton, was full of warmth and admiration in his praise of Sunil's display.

"I have had the good fortune to have seen many memorable double centuries in Test matches, and Gavaskar's 221 at the Oval in 1979 should, at the very least, be bracketed with Stan McCabe's 232 at Trent Bridge and Wally Hammond's 240 at Lord's, particularly bearing in mind the important fact that India started their second innings in the seemingly impossible position of getting 438 runs in 500 minutes to win."

In his recognition of Sunil, Hutton rated him the best batsman of either side in the series, greater than Boycott, Gooch and Gower. Hutton proudly asserted that "at his peak, he was undeniably the world's number 1."

Had India beaten England, they would have been the only team in history to win two Tests chasing over 400 runs. Australia had achieved this feat in 1948 at Headingly against England and India defeated the West Indies in 1976 at the Queen's Park Oval.

C.L.R.James, the distinguished scholar-historian, was moved by the magnificence of the achievement and expressed it in a letter to the Indian High Commissioner in Port of Spain. He recognized the effort as one of the greatest achievements in the history of cricket.

"That they picked themselves up and reached so near to winning the last Test against enormous odds will remain one of the most inspiring events in the history of this game. Many batsmen have scored more runs than Gavaskar. Not so many have so substantially established themselves in the slender role of master batsman."

James interpreted the nature of India's resistance and courageous effort as significant for India started the game with the "consciousness of unsuccessful struggle." He saw it as a struggle for assertion of one's worth, courage and pride not only against England but also other countries, and in his unique Jamesian commitment to the West Indies expressed the hope that this effort will develop "more intimate mutuality between sportsmen and people of India and their counterparts in the Caribbean."

Gavaskar was the major player in the effort. In his fertility at the turf he created his rose garden and revelled in rich sunshine, but experience at that time would have taught him that there's got to be a little "shadow" sometimes.

CHAPTER 5

Sunshine And Shadow

Yesterday,   *Success stood before you like a*
column of light, a mighty flame from
a tiny spark,
Today,   *a cloud has spread a veil that hides*
your warm and sunny laughter,
Tomorrow,   *poised between the grey mists of*
twilight and the gilded rays of dawn,
is a new hope, a new spirit, a new
vision.

Uriel Narinesingh

The majestic display which produced a vintage 221 at the Oval was an exhibition of method and skill. Wisden describes it as "technically flawless". It delighted and enthralled the English cricketing public who were so absorbed in the dramatic pursuit of 438, that it never mattered to them they were cheering on their opponents. Spectator involvement and thrill in the combat outweighed patriotic fervour for almost everyone seemed to be interested in exciting cricket, not mere outcome or results. Wisden reports that if India had won "there were many Englishmen in the crowd who would not have displayed their customary dejection at the latest defeat."

It was on such an olympian note that Gavaskar returned to India and was invited to lead the country once again. Venkataraghavan was relieved of the captaincy but he retained a place in the team. A strong opinion was expressed that Venkat's form might not have assured him a place on the team for the full series and therefore it was not prudent to retain his services as captain. Gavaskar, though proud to lead his country, at times never really cherished it. Though shrewd, knowledgeable and learned in the game, he never particularly enjoyed its responsibilities. Perhaps regional differences and the Board's strange machinations coupled with the press' intrusion were all reasons for his disinclination to lead freely. But he never singled out reasons for his lack of enthusiasm except his references to the onus of leadership.

India, during the last few months of the year 1979 were well occupied and after the English tour abroad, would be engaged in three encounters at home. A full Australian visit comprising six Tests would be followed by Pakistan in another six-Test combat. After this England would visit India for one Test to commemorate the Golden Jubilee of the formation of the Indian Board. The itinerary for 1978-79 was crowded and this meant no relaxation from the rigours of Test cricket. The 13 Test matches would take India right through to February 1980.

At this time the Packer-ICC dispute which had divided the cricket world into two camps was being addressed with some measure of clear thinking and some form of compromise was reached. But the Australian team which arrived in India was shorn of Packer players. It included Hogg, Yardley, Border, Higgs and Hughes who were to share in Australia's future cricket fortunes. India were bereft of three of their formidable spin quartet of the seventies. Prasanna, Chandrasekhar and Bedi had all faded from the cricketing scene; it was only the experienced and established Venkataraghavan from the four who had retained his place. In the series he would find new partners in Dilip Doshi and Yadav. Together with the arrival of the new spinners, Gavaskar had at his disposal Kapil Dev and Karsan Ghavri as his opening attack.

The first two Tests were interrupted and marred by rain but in each Test both teams were fairly prolific with India scoring in excess of 400 on the two occasions at the crease. On these occasions Gavaskar registered 50 and 10. His low score of ten during the second Test brought up his 5000th run in Test cricket, the first Indian to achieve this milestone. In these rain-ruined matches there were two promising debutantes. In the first Test Doshi had taken six wickets in his first innings and in the second Test N.S. Yadav's conquest yielded seven wickets.

The third Test at Kanpur was more interesting. It was played on a pitch which was surprisingly fast and it eventually experienced unexpected bounce. India, in this circumstance, managed 271 and Australia replied with 304. It was a fighting six hour innings of 84 by Chauhan which redeemed India's fortune and offered some measure of respectability to its score of 311. Gavaskar's contribution in both innings were 76 and 12. To earn victory Australia needed 279 in 312 minutes but collapsed ignominiously against Kapil Dev's fast medium swing and Yadav's off spinners. India were in the ascendancy and Gavaskar's spirit, positive and genial.

In the fourth Test at Delhi India compiled their highest score against Australia. Out of a total of 510 for 7 declared there were three centuries. Yashpal Sharma made 100 not out, Vishwanath 131 and Gavaskar scored 115, his first century of the series. Kapil Dev's penetrative 5 for 83 reduced Australia to 298 and forced a follow-on but with a determined batting effort and the help of a few dropped catches Australia saved the match. The fifth Test followed at Calcutta. Australia's effort was commendable. Hughes, the Australian captain, set India a target of 247 runs in a minimum of 245 minutes. When bad light ended play 22 balls prematurely, India were 47 short with six wickets in hand. It was a challenging battle and at the end India looked positive and like a match-winner.

Bombay was the venue for the last Test and here India ensured that they won their first series against Australia. It was a demoralizing blow for Australia with the Indian bowlers Doshi, Yadav and Kapil Dev routing their opponents. It was the most telling defeat of the series and there was more than a day to spare. India won by an innings and 100 runs thus gaining a 2-0 lead. In the process Gavaskar had scored another century in compiling 123 runs. It was his 22nd and this placed him on par with W.R. Hammond and M.C. Cowdrey. The targets ahead were Sir Gary Sobers' 26 and Sir Donald Bradman's 29 centuries.

Gavaskar had scored two centuries, 115 at Delhi and 123 at Bombay and had led India to victory. It was a memorable triumph. He evinced a quiet confidence and growing maturity in his leadership. Victory was an achievement to him, moreso, since he was unhappy with some of the selections in the team. Victory by a 2-0 margin enhanced his stature as a captain and reinforced his confidence for the following series the same winter against arch-rivals Pakistan on home soil.

The Pakistan-India series was fraught with its accustomed problems. True to tradition, these clashes usually resembled wars of attrition - dour affairs with no quarter asked or given - and this series was no exception. The final outcome reflected India's supremacy in that tour and Pakistan's fragility in defeat. Mihir Bose in his comprehensive coverage of the development of Indian cricket in "A History of Indian Cricket" remarks: "The defeat seemed to unhinge the Pakistanis. They hit out against the Indians in a disgraceful fashion. They accused Indian umpires of cheating, Indian authorities of spoiling the Bombay pitch, and Asif Iqbal talked of calling the tour off." In the six matches played India emerged 2-0 victors, winning the third Test at Bombay by 131 runs and the fifth Test at Madras by 10 wickets. The loss of the fifth Test really weakened the Pakistanis' spirit. It meant that the series was lost and their resistance weakened. Gavaskar's 166 in 593 minutes was a marathon innings and it must have afforded him great pleasure. It was the longest innings for India and later in the 1982-83 series he himself surpassed this. This century decided the outcome and with Kapil Dev in brilliant form with the bat (84) and splendid bowling (11 wickets), Pakistan could only muster 272 and 233, leaving Gavaskar and Chauhan a token target of 78 for a memorable victory. Gavaskar had scored his 23rd century and this meant that he had surpassed both Wally Hammond's and Colin Cowdrey's tally of twenty two.

After the fifth Test Gavaskar relinquished the captaincy. He was opting out of the forth-coming Caribbean tour and he thought it wise for a new leader to take over. In the sixth and final Test his brother-in-law Vishwanath was chosen for the responsibility. The West Indian tour was eventually cancelled.

The records indicate that Gavaskar did enjoy a successful series. His batting performance was impressive. He had scored 589 runs at an average of 58. Bose, in focussing on Gavaskar's contribution recalls:
"If he was at times defensive he was always in command and he had provided the essential stability the previous team lacked."

His success, while it met with great admiration from a wide majority of cricket loving supporters, did not illumine the hearts of sceptics and detractors and even some of his colleagues. When he announced his withdrawal from the West Indian tour it was felt that he was selfishly dictating his options without consideration for Indian cricket.

In February 1980, England visited India for a one-off Test to celebrate the Golden Jubilee (50 years) of the formation of the Indian Cricket Board. Though Gavaskar played in this game and scored 48 and 24, India were captained by Vishwanath. The English, led by Mike Brearley won comfortably by 10 wickets. The historic occasion witnessed a superb all-round performance by Ian Botham who, after India's innings of 242, topscored for England with a swashbuckling knock of 114 out of a total of 296 and then demolished India for 149, claiming 13 wickets for 106. It was a feat worthy of Miller, Sobers, Procter or Imran Khan!

It was in this same year of 1980 that Sunil made his debut in Somerset for his only season in English county cricket. Here he had already been acclaimed as India's first international superstar. At Somerset, he was lauded as a craftsman of a special genre who was always re-examining his methods and making adjustments to accommodate the threat of changing

The Family Cirlce - Early Years.

The Extended Family.

Sunil and Marshneil at their wedding, September 1974.

Sunil, Marshneil (Pammi) and Rohan.

Rajiv Gandhi (1983) with Sunil on the lawns of Rashtrapati Bhavan, New Delhi after the 29th Test century

Sunil meets Indian President Zail Singh.

Lord's 1971. Skipper Wadekar introduces Sunil to Queen Elizabeth of England.

President Sanjeeva Reddy presents Sunil with the Padma Bhushan Award, (1980).

Here Sunil is flanked by Sandeep Patil (right) and Hemant Waingankar (left) at a meeting during their one week visit to Trinidad in May 1995.

Sunil with Sonny Ramadin. Heroes, accomplished at different ends of the wicket, of different generations and different continents.

*Sunil with the two Rohans -
Rohan Kanhai and Rohan
Gavaskar.*

Sunil with Mother Teresa.

The two Gavaskars.
Here Sunil and son Rohan
take the field.

The year 1971.
Venue: Queen's Park Oval,
Trinidad.
Occasion: Centuries in both
innings. Here Roodal
Mahelal lifts Sunil in a
jubilant mood after his
double century at the Oval.

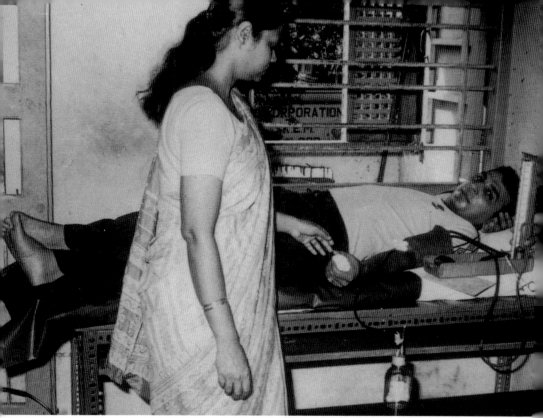

Sunil donates blood at a hospital.

Sunil addresses fans on his way to South India for a festival match.

conditions.

As a batsman with talent, Gavaskar revealed a capacity for deep concentration and well-disciplined responses, the results of a reflective and rational mind. Here he was deemed a superb batsman with a modest unassuming personality who believes that cricket is only a game and defeat is not the end of the world. To him success and failure are the results of the whims and fancies of fortune, playthings of the fates.

Sunil's ability to cope with other cricketers and to adjust to their lifestyle made him an endearing person in their company. His visit to Somerset was a treat to the Somerset folk who enjoyed his batting and found it an inspiration to the youths in their community. He succeeded in scoring a couple of centuries in county matches. His 155 not out at Weston Super Mare included three sixes and twenty fours. Against Surrey at the Oval he made 138 in 170 minutes with seventeen fours. So brilliant were his cover drives that many officials at the game were reminded of Peter May, one of England's most elegant and accomplished batsmen.

Peter Roebuck, the batsman who opened with Sunil for Somerset, articulates in his essay "Jewel of the East":
"Meeting this gentleman, it is easy to forget his marvellous Test record. That ready smile must conceal nerves of steel, for Gavaskar has scored well-nigh 6000 runs, including 23 centuries. He has formed the backbone of Indian batting for a decade. This is a country where cricket is followed with fanatical zeal, where success can bring the hazards of worship and failure the pangs of ignominy."

This is an eloquent statement of the greatness of Gavaskar's achievement at this point. The pain of ignominy and the adulation that accompany success, Gavaskar would surely experience as his career progressed.

The West Indian tour was cancelled and the Australian tour lay ahead. For this he was re-appointed captain. Again the detractors hinted that he was always favoured, that he could do no wrong and questioned the reasons for his re-appointment. It was felt that he was given the scope to dictate his course. This feeling of animosity was fuelled by inter-state rivalry which focussed on Gavaskar, the Bombay hero, as inward-looking and parochial.

Bombay had been traditionally viewed as "one of the most important power centres of the game." But in the late seventies and early eighties there was a challenge from the northern states with cricketers staking strong claims for Test selection. In the 1979-80 Ranji Trophy season, the northern players made an impact on state cricket. In the top twenty places there were eight players from the North. The North also boasted of three top class bowlers. But in the Indian tour to Australia and New Zealand during the 1980-81 season, according to Mihir Bose, "this northern dominance was not reflected". Out of seventeen players only five from the North were selected. This led to discontent and though Gavaskar had always represented the interest of cricketers, it was felt that he was partial to Bombay. Critics felt that Gavaskar simply addressed his attention to Bombay players to the exclusion of others.

In an article entitled "The Decline of Indian Cricket" Pataudi attempted to analyse the resistance to Gavaskar.
"Gavaskar was the greatest, and while no one doubted this, it is plain that only some Bombay players paid him sycophantic homage. Perhaps the others were jealous but no matter how hard he tried, many cricketers from elsewhere were unable to give him their full trust. They felt that Gavaskar stood for Gavaskar though he had often clashed with the authorities for the benefit of his team."

It was felt that he was 'stealing the limelight' gaining the publicity and the money. His ascent was amazing and all others looked insignificant. But in fact, he had seriously acted in the interest of the cricketers and even got in conflict with the Board.

Bose recognized that Gavaskar had done more for Indian cricketers than any other player. And in terms of performance as captain, before the Australian and New Zealand tours he was outstanding. The West Indies, Australia and Pakistan were all dethroned by his team at home. In 1980-81, though not successful with the bat, he had drawn the series against Australia and lost one match to New Zealand. During his twenty four Test tenure, he had lost two and won six Tests. In capturing the true spirit of the times, the enigmas and the complexities that surrounded the Gavaskar legend, Bose saw him as the besieged hero.

India's schedule on the international level was a busy one. In this 1980-81 season Gavaskar led the team 'Down Under' to measure swords with Australia, now led by the brilliant batsman, Greg Chappell, and having in its ranks players of the highest calibre like Walters, Border, Marsh and Lillee. India's team was largely unchanged, with Sandeep Patil, Doshi and Ghavri seeking to consolidate their places and Gavaskar and Kapil Dev still the leading lights.

The tour was disappointing for India and it was not destined to be a happy or successful one for Sunil. Though the three Tests series was shared one all, his personal batting performance was well below his accustomed standard and he failed to score one of his customary centuries. Worse than this, he was directly involved in one of his most controversial incidents in a career that was known for its clashes and confrontations.

Australia won the opening Test at Sydney by an innings with Greg Chappell scoring an imperious 204 in an Australian total of 406. India made 201 in both innings with Sunil having an every once in a while double failure, being caught behind off Lillee for a duck in the first innings and out for 10 in the second innings. As so often happened whenever he was dismissed early, India's fortunes plummeted as Lillee bagged seven wickets in the match with only Patil topping 50. The second Test at Adelaide ended in a draw in the home team's favour; Gavaskar failed again (23 and 5) and though Patil batted courageously for 174 in an innings of "raw power, rare charm and an enviable elegance", a double century by Hughes had put the Aussies firmly in command and at the denouement of the match, India barely escaped with a draw at 135 for 8. It was a grim struggle with Ghavri and Yadav doing yeoman service to their country by staving off defeat.

Khalid Ansari writing in "Sportsweek's" "How Come India?" points to Gavaskar's serious predicament. He had entered Australia on this occasion with a great reputation and expectations were high. Both India and Australia saw his development as positive; but here, his performance lacked the usual lustre, discipline and concentration. He realized concentration was his problem but was not able to work out the reason for his lapses.

"I have never had lapses like this in Tests. Perhaps I am playing too many shots too early. I have had concentration problems before, but never in Tests."

It was only in the final Test that the crowd began to see glimpses of the true master at his craft. His second innings score of 70 was one of concentration and diligence. He himself seemed pleased with his performance until it was rudely interrupted by a decision which almost triggered off one of the most controversial events in the history of Test cricket had not the Indian manager intervened.

All the critics immediately put pen to paper and echoed what Don Mosey wrote in this extract:

"Gavaskar took his captaincy very seriously indeed; to such an extent that he came close to an international incident which could have had the most disastrous consequences for him and for Indian cricket."

In this final Test India had made 237 with the main contribution from Vishwanath (114 runs). Again Gavaskar had failed. In reply Australia had amassed another formidable score of 419. Faced with a huge deficit of 182 India started their final innings. It was in this innings that Gavaskar and Chauhan enjoyed a 165 opening partnership. He was batting with calm and composure until Lillee produced a ball which Gavaskar was confident he had edged. Lillee appealed and the umpire complied by adjudging him LBW. Gavaskar's anger was further provoked by Lillee's profanities and in this mood Gavaskar called on Chauhan to withdraw from the match and proceed to the pavilion. Chauhan was persuaded by the manager to return to the crease before he could enter the pavilion. This incident which was slightly short of being explosive is reviewed in a later chapter in this work.

Play continued with India posting 324 on the scoreboard and inviting Australia to pursue a meagre 143 for victory. The Indian camp appeared grim and bleaky since three of the bowlers, Kapil, Doshi and Yadav were at a disadvantage through injury. But in spite of this they struggled and with determination and strength of will were able to frustrate Australia's hope of victory. India had bowled out Australia for 83 runs, with Kapil Dev claiming 5 for 43 in a superb spell.

India had almost forfeited the Test and the ironic thing about that whole incident is that they eventually won the match by 59 runs to level the series at 1-1. It was a dramatic match and an incredible feat in the light of Australian dominance which characterized the series. However, the end was no indication of who truly enjoyed the glory.

Shortly after the visit to Australia, the Indian team made a visit to New Zealand. The euphoria of the Melbourne triumph soon gave way to utter shock and disenchantment when the lowly Kiwis, then the cinderellas of the Test match arena, with only John Wright, Geoff Howarth, Hadlee and Coney of undisputed Test quality, convincingly won at Wellington by 62 runs. India were routed for 223 and 190, with Gavaskar experiencing failures. His innings in three Tests put together totalled 126 with 53 being his highest score and an average of 25.20. After New Zealand's victory in the first Test, rain ruined the second encounter and it was only in the last innings of the final Test that the Indian bowlers showed New Zealand some semblance of their capabilities. The match however ended in a draw and the Kiwis had gained their first series win over India.

As a result of the injuries to Doshi and Yadav, Gavaskar called on his Bombay colleague, the youthful Ravi Shastri, to do duty. This again provoked the critics to mutter that Gavaskar was giving preferential treatment to his state. They viewed it as a plot to frustrate players such as Rajendra Goel who had made a great impact in domestic cricket. But Shastri did perform very creditably in his first Test series and the choice did indicate Gavaskar's cricketing shrewdness and intelligence. Though the critics were at his throat, Shastri's performance did silence them for a while. It is interesting to note that Gavaskar has selected Rajendra Goel as one of his idols though he has never played Test cricket. He held great admiration for Goel's cricketing ability but felt that Bedi's presence on the scene left no room in Test cricket for either Goel or Padmakar Shivalkar, another of his idols. In the situation described, it is not difficult to understand Goel's absence and Shastri's presence. To lend more credibility to Gavaskar's stance, it can be argued that Shastri's youth contributed to his Test claim.

Personal failure and his team's disastrous performance left him a sad and dejected man. He was a man whose genial spirit failed and in the process he experienced a strange sense of loneliness. Though a man of strength and courage, failure for him was fraught with tension and trauma. He remarked: "I was always frightened of failure. The team relied on me a lot, and the crowds expected me to succeed."

The demands of performing with consistency did take a toll on him. Since his dramatic entry into the Test arena and his unique successes, expectations for him had been great. The forces which surrounded him and impinged on his consciousness were too selfish to realize that his humanness did not allow for the perfection they expected of him. The Indians had done more harm to him and had he not been cushioned by the love and dedication of his wife and parental care together with the healthy support of his friends, he would have been unable to lift the 'smothering weight' from his thoughts and inner self.

On his return from the Australian and New Zealand tours he was alert to his friends' responses and reactions.
"When I came back from Australia in 1981, I thought my friends might not treat me the same way. But I found my friends and those who mattered to me were still the same. That brought a change in my attitude and I began to enjoy the game a lot more after that. To that point I was involved only for success and cricket was the only thing. Cricket is still the major thing in my life, but it is not the only thing."

The realization that a supportive family and true friendship are of great sustenance, especially when one is faced with adversity and failure, inspired him and he examined himself. It was to him a great discovery that there are beauteous forms of life which are engaging and fulfilling and that meant more than winning or losing. He was heartened by the warmth and fellowship which prevailed. He reflected:
"If you have good friends, and if you have a supporting family, then nothing can happen to you."

Gavaskar surprisingly escaped the selectors' axe for the next home series against England in 1982. It was another six Test programme. It was largely a high scoring rubber, nine centuries being scored with five totals in excess of 400. It was mostly due to the batting efforts of the dapper Indian skipper Gavaskar together with Kapil Dev, Vishwanath and Doshi that India salvaged a slender 1-0 victory in the series. Gavaskar's only century, of 172, came in the second Test at Bangalore but he passed 50 on three other occasions, batting at times in excellent rein and with panache and belligerence. At Bombay, where his team won by 138 runs, he made 55 and later Kapil and Madan Lal routed Keith Fletcher's side for 102. Both bowled effectively against England who complained bitterly of the standard of the umpiring.

Five consecutive draws followed including a high scoring one at Delhi where at 46 he missed out on a run feast and then hit 83 not out at Calcutta. Botham and Kapil Dev both got centuries in the final Test when rain and bad light ruined the match. Incidentally, at Bangalore Gavaskar was on the field for all but four balls of the game! His series aggregate was 500 runs with an average of 62, but he came in for some more flak for his defensive tactics from the English press, during a tour riddled with political controversy because of the South African connection. At one stage the tour itself was in danger of being cancelled.

India toured England again in 1982, sharing the summer with Pakistan. Gavaskar was at the helm this time and he may have had fond hopes of victory in the Test series against a weakened English team (a rebel party to South Africa had been banned from international cricket for three years). But India had an unbalanced attack. Kapil Dev had little pace support and the batsmen usually failed to click, except Dilip Vengsarkar who hit a century at Lord's, a match England won by seven wickets.

Gavaskar's scores in the three Test series were 48, 24 and 2. He was unable to bat in the final match at the Oval, because fielding at silly point while Botham played a pyrotechnic innings of savage brilliance, compiling his highest Test score of 208, Sunil was struck a fearsome blow which fractured his left fibula. Both that Test and the match at Old Trafford were left drawn, England compiling 594 at the London venue. It had been a truly sad tour for Gavaskar whose expectations had been high. Controversy dogged him relentlessly. As skipper, he objected to the inclusion of David Constant on the panel of arbiters, despite his high reputation as an umpire. He had been critical of Constant in the 1971 tour for his partiality to English players. Now Gavaskar's critics castigated him for his stance, terming it a malicious ploy.

Late in 1983, India met Sri Lanka in the inaugural Test at Madras between the two countries. In his first major match, since suffering a fractured shin, Gavaskar hammered an attractive 155, his 25th Test century, which formed the backbone of a mammoth Indian total of 506 for 6 declared, in which Patil also scored an unbeaten 114. Although they led Sri Lanka by 220 on the first innings, Duleep Mendis, the Sri Lankan batsman, scored centuries in both innings and in the end, India were struggling to stave off an improbable defeat at 135 for 7, an embarrassing display against the newly initiated Test team. Fortunately, a strained neck forced Gavaskar to demote himself to number 9 in the batting lineup, and he and Yashpal Sharma held firm, though not without some alarms.

The next series of the same year was an Indian tour to Pakistan. The events and outcome of this tour were difficult for the Indians to digest. In the previous encounter of 1979-80 Pakistan found it difficult to come to terms with the loss they experienced. Here in 1983, a drawn first Test, defeat in the second by an innings and 86 runs, a ten wicket defeat in the third Test, another calamitous crushing by an innings and 119 runs were enough to demoralize the Indians. The final two Tests were drawn.

It was a powerful side led by Imran Khan, and it included Zaheer Abbas, Javed Miandad and Mudassar Nazar, all in prolific batting form. The Pakistani batsmen blossomed and flourished. There were innings in excess of 400. In the first four Tests, scores of 485, 452, 652, 581 for 3 declared firmly established Pakistani's batting supremacy. Imran was in a devastating mood with the new ball, claiming 11 wickets at both Karachi and Faisalabad and collecting 40 wickets in the series. India found little to console them for their attack was limited in comparison, apart from Kapil Dev's 8 wickets in an innings at Lahore. It was only Mohinder Amarnath, who was included in this series and also Gavaskar who played with confidence and assurance. Amarnath emerged with a remarkable record of 584 runs at an average of 73. The Indian veteran and opener and skipper, now aged 33, totalled 434 at an average of 48 and scored a fine 127 not out in a total of 286 at Faisalabad; but it was to no avail. He had batted to the end of the innings or 'carried his bat' as in cricketing jargon such an innings is described. It was his 26th Test century. He was now on par with Sir Gary and it was only the legendary Sir Don Bradman, with a record 29 Test centuries to his credit, who remained at the top of the list.

India had to do some serious assessment of their performance and their stature in the international arena. In the bowling department, Doshi clearly showed that he was past his prime, though he would not admit his shortcoming. In addition to this Vishwanath's performance was most disturbing. His was a dismal failure, though a great loss when he was excluded from the Indian tour in subsequent tours. It was a loss to Indian cricket and a greater loss to international cricket for here was the end of the Test career of a truly great batsman. But the cricketing world had been the richer for having him.

The devastating blow to Gavaskar's team is reminiscent of the defeat Bedi suffered at the hands of Pakistan in 1978-79. The same fate that awaited Bedi also beckoned Gavaskar. The Indian team were outplayed by their arch-rivals, and it was predictable that his job as captain would be on the line when the team returned home. A trouncing by Pakistan is always far more unpalatable to Indian tastes than defeat at the hands of England, Australia or the West Indies. National pride demands sacrifice and the first head to roll is usually the captain's. Gavaskar was relieved of the captaincy but was invited to tour the Caribbean in the next series as a player.

It is significant to note that after his great display of technical excellence and dominance which was clearly seen in his innings of 221 in England, and his successes both as captain and batsman over Australia and Pakistan, there were fluctuations in his performances. He had failed in Australia and New Zealand in 1981, but was triumphant over Fletcher's English team at home though it was not a dynamic series. The visit which followed the Pakistan tour to England lacked prosperity. A growing sense of unease and dissatisfaction in the Indian camp did not help. Dilip Doshi felt his bowling skill was not well exploited. Earlier on he complained of having to bowl in Australia when he had suffered a fracture. To this Gavaskar replied that he was unaware of it. Dissatisfaction had reared its ugly head when the North felt that Gavaskar had preferred players like Suru Nayah and Ghulam Parkar for the English tour when Mohinder Amarnath was in excellent batting form. In response to the complaint he admitted that they did not perform creditably but in the same breath pointed out that neither did Gursharan Singh nor Ashok Malhotra give a good account of themselves. To counter his critics he indicated that these two were from the North and "did someone accuse Kapil of having been parochial?"

In terms of records as a captain he had not truly failed; he had brought glory to his team against Australia, England, Pakistan and the West Indies during his tenure. Should he take all the responsibility if his batsmen and bowlers were under-achievers in Pakistan? Or could he have inspired and motivated them more to perform creditably and save humiliation against the opposition? Did he lack the determination and will to conquer and win? All these issues were raised at the end of the series which they lost 2-0. His defensive tactics were often open to criticism. It was muttered in some quarters that he could have won the West Indian series in 1978 at home by a more convincing margin if he had possessed the killer instinct. But then in 1983 on the Pakistan tour of India he did show his dynamism by inspiring his team to a splendid 2-0 victory over a team which appeared superior in both batting and bowling. A closer and more detailed review of his captaincy appears in a later chapter in this work.

India had not won a Test match since in Bombay in December 1982 when the time approached to pick the team for what would be a hard and gruelling tour to the Caribbean, their fifth to the West Indies. Since that time, under Gavaskar's captaincy they had lost four Tests and drawn eleven and understandably the selectors now opted for a change in leadership. Gavaskar was, of course, named in the touring party; but the young burgeoning lion, Kapil Dev, aptly nicknamed the 'Haryana Hurricane' by his admirers, was elevated to the captaincy at the age of 24 and Gavaskar's claims overlooked.

Throughout their careers this duo was destined to be strong rivals. Sunil, the pride of Bombay, was a specialist opening batsman with honours already heaped thick upon him; a man who had ushered in a renaissance in Indian cricket and only Bradman had hit more centuries at Test cricket level than him with 29 to Sunil's 26; the crowning showpiece of the game's devotees. On the other hand, Kapil Dev was a very promising all-rounder who had already demonstrated his exciting prowess as a belligerent middle-order batsman, athletic fieldsman and explosive paceman; easily India's most menacing pace bowler since the halcyon pre-war days of Amar Singh. The personalities, gifts and temperaments of these two men were as different as chalk and cheese. Two qualities though, they shared in common...... charisma and supreme faith in themselves. On the cricket field they oozed confidence at every pore. They abhorred mediocrity, scoffed at adversity or a challenge and thumbed their noses at misfortune. They both provided a welcome tonic for Indian cricket, too often bogged down in anaemic batting methods and succumbing with no real resistance to the Scylla of speed; whether it was Trueman, Lillee or the West Indian pace brigade. The media, of course, always promoted the fallacy that both Sunil and Kapil were sworn enemies for this made 'good copy'.

It was a revolutionary change made by the selectors for the Caribbean tour, but clearly they felt that the time was ripe for new leadership to change India's luck and improve her Test fortunes. The loss in Pakistan had been most galling and humiliating; so a gamble was taken.

The stewardship of Gavaskar had not worked despite his intrinsic batting skill and now the nod, the vote of confidence went to northern India, Kapil Dev's domain. The perennial pendulum had swung back to a new idol, India's response

continent in 1983-84, an India-Pakistan contest ended in a stalemate. In the Bangalore Test, very little separated the teams on first innings, and later Gavaskar scored his 28th century, sharing an unbroken stand with Anshuman Gaekwad. This was, by the way, the first Test match in which 'no-balls' and 'wides' were debited to bowlers' analyses.

Jullundur was the venue for the second match, becoming the 55th Test centre. In reply to Pakistan's total of 337, India made 374 with Gaekwad slamming 201. Gavaskar was bowled for 5 in a game marred by rain; but at Nagpur he scored 50 and 64 topscoring in the second innings, while Zaheer Abbas batted superbly for 85. This was the third clash between these countries in which every Test was undecided and at times the series bordered on being farcical and pedestrian in its tempo.

A strong West Indian team opposed India in a six Test series between October and November 1983. The visitors extracted sweet revenge for their shocking defeat in the World Cup in England earlier in the year, winning three Test matches and drawing the others, in all of which India led on first innings and more than held their own. Kapil Dev was again captain and though he had a lean series with the bat, he bowled magnificently throughout, capturing 29 wickets at 18 runs a piece. Both Marshall (33) and Holding (30) bettered this but Andy Roberts had to be content with a mere five wickets and seemed over the hill.

Gavaskar enjoyed excellent batting form, totalling 505 runs, while Lloyd (496) and Greenidge starred for the visitors. India lost heavily at Kanpur in the first match where Greenidge scored a brilliant 194 and Marshall made his best Test score of 92 in a total of 454. Gavaskar failed twice here, but at Delhi his sparkling and belligerent 121 equalled Bradman's record of 29 hundreds. India led by 80 on the first innings but the match petered out and the home side had now not savoured victory for 25 matches, a national record. The West Indies pacemen ensured victory by 138 runs at Ahmedabad where Gavaskar continued in dynamic style in accumulating 90 fluent runs. He did little in the drawn Bombay Test and the elusive 30th century never came at Calcutta. And this proved disastrous.

His 30th Test century was becoming more and more urgent, if not for Sunil, for the crowd's happiness. Ahmedabad's effort was not fully sustained and Bombay brought no success. Calcutta had always been a favourite venue but never a significantly successful one. There was a growing urgency, both on his part and the crowd's for a grand performance. Now the time was most opportune. Sunil recalls in "Runs 'n Ruins":
"Their fervour was touching and I prayed that I should be able to fulfil their wishes."

But the Gods were not smiling on him as he made the briefest of engagements at the crease. The crowd's ambition and hope for a grand, heroic exhibition intensified the pressures and anxiety which he was experiencing. Though he always asserted that we are the 'playthings of the fates' and that winning and losing are inconsequential, his commitment as a sportsman to his countrymen was the overriding concern. They actually entered his consciousness, searched his inner being with an overwhelming passion and in so doing looked to him for glory and honour.

In the second innings he attempted to make amends and started favourably, flicking and driving Marshall to the delight of a cheering crowd. With the adrenaline flowing he negotiated a wide outswinger from Holding and square drove it uppishly for four. He was getting into his aggressive stride and repeated a square drive off Holding only to snick the ball to Dujon with his score on 20. That was the end; a dismal one. He chastised himself for a 'terrible shot,' "a stupid waste of a wicket and a complete letdown," and recalls the anguish of that moment:
"I returned to the pavilion with my ears ringing with cries of anguish, rather than with abuse of the crowd."

In anger he felt that he had disappointed so many waiting to witness a stupendous record and now what he had done 'was shockingly irresponsible'. The crowd's anger began to surface and he felt their behaviour was justified. The pressure of the circumstances led to lack of will power, failure of spirit and his main solace and sustenance as has always been, was his wife Pammi. She had always been an inspiring force in his life and her support was immeasurable. The greater consolation lay in the fact that during the eighties wives were not excluded from tours and her presence and support eased his dejection.

During the course of the match the volatile and fickle spectators, angered at their hero's demise and the team's failures, were incensed. Their wrath was directed at him and the other cricketers in a violent manner. But what terrified and maddened him was their attack on Pammi. They had begun to throw fruit and rubbish at her. He was prepared for their onslaught to be directed at him, but was alarmed at their unfeeling, callous and vulgar display.

Sunil left Calcutta with a 'heavy heart' and 'his confidence at a pretty low ebb'. He was made to feel guilty, and it was as if an 'albatross was hung around his neck'. But in the final encounter at Madras he presented himself though with reluctance and it was here that the elusive 30th century became a reality. Batting at number 4, a drop in the batting order which he had requested, Sunil compiled a monumental 236 not out. This eclipsed his 221 at the Oval as his best performance statistically. It contained 23 fours and he batted for 644 minutes. The only apparent blemish was experienced when there was a close call for a catch. He was adjudged not out much to the chagrin and dismay of his adversaries. But his strokeplay was polished, his defence impregnable, as the bowlers toiled in vain.

Gavaskar had again proved his mettle in this series with only Amarnath topping him in the batting averages. For the moment the diminutive opener savoured his unbeaten double century as the season ended. And when India toured Pakistan in 1984, Bombay had regained the 'ascendancy' with Gavaskar back at the helm for what proved to be a short high scoring series.

He received a congratulatory cable from Sir Donald Bradman after his Madras performance, an admirable gesture from the Don. Few critics knew then that he would garner four more test centuries before he finally retired with a total of 10,122 runs; a record that stood until Border eclipsed it in the 1990's.

It was his fourth double century at Test match level and his third against the West Indies. So after a brief 'drought' on the 1983 tour to the Caribbean, Sunil had again demonstrated his relish for West Indian bowling! The Windies' attack at Madras included a formidable pace quartet in Marshall, Roberts, Holding and Davis, supported by off spinner Harper. It is a tribute to Gavaskar's innate skill that he was still able to prosper against this calibre of hostile bowling. His landmark achievement in his 99th Test made banner headlines throughout the Commonwealth, not least in the "Bombay Times", as Indian hearts surged with justifiable national pride.

CHAPTER 6

Harvest Of Achievement

*And now the matchless deeds achieved
Determined, Dared and Done.*

Christopher Smart: Song of David

Gavaskar had completed his 28th Test century and was on the verge of equalling the much coveted magnificent record of 29 centuries held by Sir Donald Bradman. Failures on the Caribbean Tour and the Prudential World Cup in 1983, followed by his disastrous Kanpur first Test failure against the West Indies led to unease and a loss of confidence. But on many occasions in his career after experiences of failure and its attendant anguish and agony, he was reputed for his ability to repair his ruins and restore his distinctive image as an outstanding craftsman. Here in the midst of cynicism, indignation, rivalries, he knew in his heart and through that indefinable force that determines one's actions, that he had to assert his presence once more and accomplish further feats of greatness.

It was felt that the incessant barrage of fast bowling affected him and his concentration had weakened. In an article entitled: "Wanted...Runs from the Maestro" Ashis Ray asserts:
"He has withstood the danger and incisiveness inherent in this type of bowling with a finesse and fortitude few can match in the long and lustrous catalogue of the game. But he might have been confronted by too much quick bowling, and much too constantly, by virtue of which he developed chinks in his concentration.....one of his assets."

Faced with tremendous pace bowling as he led from the front, coupled with the rigours of Test cricket, he admitted that he was experiencing some difficulty with his technique and concentration. In the Caribbean tour of 1983 he seemed to succumb to the fiery pace of Marshall etc, though in his defence one must recall his century in Guyana and his 90 in a one-day international and also acknowledge that some very good deliveries accounted for his dismissals. The West Indians in that tour, so familiar with his successes of the two previous visits in 1971 and 1976, seemed to have targeted him as the main threat and never allowed him freedom to continue in his glorious path. Then there was the first Test at Kanpur. There was reason for concern and the critics were advocating his dismissal from the scene. His close associate, Vasu Paranjpe advised that he counter the attack, for he knew that Sunil possessed the technique, skill and experience. His psychological advantage of mastery of fast bowling was in his favour if he dared to counter attack. With this in mind he approached the second Test in true combative spirit.

Gavaskar at once gave the impression that he was not going to subject himself to humiliation or to the terrors of pace in a defensive manner. In the first over he missed perilously while attempting a square cut. He then hooked Marshall for four off the first ball of the second over. The aggression and hostility of the first half hour was met with positive response from him. He was defiant, daring and adventurous in his strategy. In a dynamic display of aggression he warmed the hearts of the enraptured crowd and shocked the confident and equally aggressive West Indian brigade. He seemed a man truly enjoying his cricket, though the critics forever at his throat, were willing to label him as the reckless, wanton aggressor.

In the twelfth over his fifty came with a boundary. He had faced 37 balls. He had hooked Marshall for a six and then sent Holding's delivery straight to the boundary as well, this time though for a well deserved four. When Davis entered the fray, Gavaskar despatched his first two deliveries for fours, a brilliant drive followed by a square cut. Vengsarkar joined him in a positive mood and he then plundered Holding for ten in one over after surviving an LBW appeal. Marshall then decided to go around the wicket and was hit for four. He then pulled Marshall's next delivery from off-side to midwicket. The battle intensified as Marshall accelerated and Gavaskar rose to the occasion with a delightful square cut, unparalleled amongst the day's boundaries. Mudhar Patherya reports: "Gavaskar's was an awesome innings. His switch to aggression had become increasingly noticeable."

In the 94th ball he faced he drove Marshall for his 100th run and this century brought him on par with Don Bradman's 29th century record. It was a moment of great historical significance when he faced the crowd; both performer and audience full of emotion. His innings came to an end at 121.

In describing the events of the day in his book "Runs 'N Ruins" he recalls:
"Everytime Marshall bounced I hooked." He had been enjoying his performance because "the ball was coming through nicely and one could play shots without worrying about movement off the wicket."
His command at the crease was imposing "for the ball went off like an obedient thing when told to do so."

Of that historic moment of his achievement on the pitch at Delhi he says "It was a benumbing moment." It was an occasion he greatly cherished and was pleased that it brought satisfaction and filled the hearts of the many well-wishers who were morally supportive when he was experiencing the trauma of failure. Sunil felt he had brought joy to them; their expectations were urgent and strong and though it enhanced his self-esteem, he felt compelled to fulfill the desires of his supportive countrymen. His honest and sincere thoughts and feelings are expressed in the following lines:
"It was therefore a great relief to get that century and see the delight on the faces of my countrymen. They had waited for it patiently, prayed for it and probably had tension in their lives while I was struggling for it. There is simply no way I can express my gratitude to the Indian cricket lovers

for the way they supported, encouraged and at times chided me during my career. I imagine the only thing I can do to repay their loving concern is to try and score as many runs as I can before Test cricket is finished with me."

The 29th Test century and his 90 which followed in the third Test at Ahmedabad also seemed to be responses to those critics who viewed him only as an orthodox batsman with a defensive approach to his craft and who had forgotten the flourishes, elegance and dynamic presence of his 1971 debut. His defensive style over the years, as has been repeatedly expressed, was determined by need and purpose, but his repertoire of strokes was always evident. His later years during the period 1984 to 1987 were expressive of his more relaxed approach to the game which brought thrilling strokes off the bat.

Pataudi, in his analysis of the Delhi match writes:
"He was determined to play most of the strokes in his considerable repertoire, including the rarely displayed hook and soon Marshall was dispelled from the attack. It has been noticeable in the past season or two, that Gavaskar's tactics have been to attack the bowling at the beginning of the innings and then settle down after scoring 30 or 40 runs. There was no decrease in the tempo this time and his 29th century was also one of the most entertaining to have come from his bat."

Scyld Berry, writing on Gavaskar's performance against the West Indies in "Sportsweek" remarks that "Gavaskar was castigated (like Boycott) but he saw the light not too late in life, unveiled his strokes, vented his talent, and gave pleasure to general spectators as well as his committed followers." Berry recognized that his last few years were spent in 'top gear' and his innings at Delhi and Ahmedabad were memorable with strokeplay of the purest brilliance. The only comparison he can make with those innings is Hutton's vignette 37 at Sydney in the 1946-47 tour.

Marshneil, (Sunil's wife) in her elation saw these innings as a response to those who were over-critical of his lean period of batting.

Gavaskar, in assessing his 29th century rated it as his second best effort. He is still emphatic that his century at Manchester in 1974 was his best. He also felt it was not fair to call his 29th century a record; it was more of an achievement of which he felt proud and full of pride as an Indian.

The Indian crowd was now in a state of euphoria. Their hero had asserted his presence in the cricketing world with honour now more than ever and this was recognized by both his contemporaries and his adversaries. The mood of the crowd was mixed.....there was patience blended with impatience, animated expectancy and compelling attentiveness; there was memory and desire as his countrymen waited for the greater event in cricket history ...... his achievement of the new record..... the 30th Test century.

Gavaskar, more than anyone else, knew the compelling nature of this feat. His tense moments were experienced not simply through his desire to bring to fruition the crowning glory of his career, but were largely due to his sensitivity to the expectations and yearnings of his supporters. And he did experience periods of anxiety before his ascent to the cricketing Everest. After his sparkling display at Ahmedabad, when he got close to the 30th century, his aggression did not work well for him. In the Test at Calcutta his dramatic start in the same aggressive mood ended abruptly through indiscretion in his strokeplay. A disappointed Calcutta crowd was incensed by their hero's 'folly' and expressed their wrath visibly.

The spirit that pervaded in Madras was encouraging and conducive to success. "It was such a pleasure to play in Madras," Sunil recalls. He had always enjoyed his stay there, the efficiency of the administration and the warmth of the reception. And he was happy that "the crowds are well behaved and respect your privacy; and are unfailingly courteous and polite. It made the player less tense and thus able to concentrate on his game that much more."

At Madras, Sunil batted in his usual exemplary manner. Partab

Ramchand in his report on the final Test writes:
"Gavaskar's batting slowly gathered rhythm and momentum. The way he made those wristy turns to square leg and played the ball beautifully off his toes, he already seemed good enough for a century and beyond."

His century did come. It was his 99th Test appearance and his record breaking 30th Test century. Lloyd's efforts to unnerve him did not succeed as Gavaskar compiled runs with 'meticulous efficiency'. The memory of two Test centuries in his three previous Tests at this stadium was fresh and he seemed eager to build on those precious moments. He cover drove Harper and Davis, then glanced Davis to fine leg. A strike to square leg off Harper brought him to 99 and then a wristy turn forward of square took him to the summit. It was his 30th Test century. It included 10 fours during a stay of 270 minutes and in which he faced 183 deliveries. The thunderous applause and ovation would linger in the memory. This century seemed to have motivated him for he continued batting and eventually surpassed his highest score of 221 and finally ended at 236 not out.

Observers record that though it was his highest score and a record breaking one, it did not compare with the flair and sparkling, entertaining quality of his 29th century or the masterful expression of his technical excellence at the Oval when he scored his 221 or any other of his memorable innings he had played. This observation does not imply that his 30th century was deficient in craftsmanship, but that, according to the critics, it did not measure up to some of his greater innings.
His display here indicated and signified that at 34 years he was still in command and could blend harmoniously aggression and defence, a virtue in his craft which Raj Singh Dungarpur proudly commended. This series against the West Indies confirmed his mastery and his continuing ability to face the strongest pace attack with skill and method. In the role of a great sportsman he was able to resist the pressures of

adversarial combat and emerge heroic. It is this skill and method and technique to negotiate pace with success that truly define a batsman of distinction.

राष्ट्रपति
भारत गणतंत्र
PRESIDENT
REPUBLIC OF INDIA

October 30, 1983

My dear Gavaskar,

    I congratulate you for your outstanding success in scoring the 29th century in International Test Cricket and in becoming a record holder with legendary world cricketer, Sir Donald Bradman.

    It was a sight to see you batting yesterday which I enjoyed every minute of my stay there. From the word go you had gone into attack without ever looking back, with masterful strokes in all directions, which speaks of your skill in the game. The importance of your achievement is in the fact that for the first time an Indian cricketer has established a record in the world cricket. I am sure that this feat will inspire all other players and take the game to new heights.

    I wish you good luck in future.

Yours sincerely,

(ZAIL SINGH)

Shri Sunil Gavaskar,
C/o D.D.C.A.,
New Delhi.

Inevitably, the pundits of the game, students of cricket history and countless armchair critics have deemed it obligatory to compare Australia's batting maestro Sir Don Bradman and Sunil Gavaskar.

Their presence has enriched the game and informed it with a blend of craftmanship that not only reveals its aesthetic quality, but also provides interest, pleasure and entertainment. Both the Don and the Little Master are living legends and household names in the rich mosaic of the game, adulated by millions throughout the British Commonwealth, regardless of the critics' nationality or patriotic persuasion. It is therefore quite natural and in the fitness of things that critics will indulge in analyses and comparisons of their careers.

Though Gavaskar was an opening batsman (until the twilight of his dazzling career, on occasion) and Bradman usually batted for his country at number 3, the cumulative effect of their statistical achievements - to say nothing of their charisma, personalities and superb mastery of technique and circumstance - almost makes it mandatory that a comparison between these two superlative batsmen be attempted and their careers in Test cricket be analysed for the sake of posterity.

In the 118 years of Test matches, the pair have, individually scored more centuries than any other batsman: the Indian titan made 34 between 1971 and 1987, while the Australian hero garnered 29 in a career spanning the period 1928-1948. It is pertinent, though, to bear in mind - if our comparison is to be objective - that while Gavaskar made his Test hundreds in no fewer than 214 innings (125 matches) all told, Bradman did so in only 80 encounters at the crease and a mere 52 Tests. That is surely an awesome statistic, attesting to the marvellous consistency of this genius of the willow. More than this, when Gavaskar equalled the Don's final tally of 29 centuries (on that momentous occasion at Delhi versus the West Indies on October 29,1983 when he scored 121 off only 94 balls) it was his 166th innings and 95th Test. In stark contrast, Bradman reached his last century -173 not out against

England at Leeds 1948 in 79 innings and only 51 matches.

Both, of course, were prolific batsmen and the star player of their respective countries. But in the matter of double centuries Gavaskar hit four at Test level while Bradman made 12 and he outstrips India's maestro, too, when we compare their final Test average: Gavaskar at 51.12 and the Don at 99.94. This in itself may not be conclusive but it illustrates the latter's phenomenal dominance over opposing bowlers. In terms of percentages, Bradman again takes dominance, scoring a century in 36 percent of his knocks; Gavaskar in 15 percent.

It would be relevant, also, to remember that Bradman batted throughout his illustrious career in an era of uncovered pitches, while Gavaskar played his cricket in the modern age when it was mandatory to cover the wicket as an insurance against bad weather. Few critics really appreciate the immensity of this difference in relative cricket conditions.

It may be asked: what of the calibre of the respective top bowlers they each faced during their careers? In this regard, both men emerge with distinction since both scored runs in generous amounts against the best bowling attacks. It would be a bold critic who would state that either enjoyed a distinct advantage, because he faced an inferior galaxy of names. Bradman had to contend with names like Larwood, Voce, Tate, Bowes, Verity, Peebles, (all English), Constantine and Herman Griffith of the West Indies and later, after the war, Vinoo Mankad and Alec Bedser. They were all excellent exponents of the bowling art. Nor were all pre-war pitches benign and comatose, by any standards. He also met and conquered Grimmet, O'Reilly and Tim Wall in Sheffield Shield domestic cricket 'Down Under'.

Gavaskar, for his part, crossed swords at Test level during the period 1971-1987 with great bowlers like Lillee, Thomson, Hogg (Australia), Snow, Willis, Botham (England), Hadlee of New Zealand; Imran Khan (Pakistan) as well as a dazzling array of West Indian firepower, propelled by outstanding pacemen such as Holding, Roberts, Garner, Croft, Marshall, Clarke, in addition to the probing spin of Lance Gibbs and the versatile Sobers. He scored Test centuries against all countries including Sri Lanka. Both of them prospered richly against this assembly of fine bowlers in their heyday.

It must be said, that a comparison of these two gifted batsmen, is in reality an exercise in futility. Certain epithets come readily to mind when analysing the greatness of Bradman. He was in a sense, a batting machine and the cricket world had never seen his like when he burst upon the Test Scene against England in 1928. Not even Grace or Hammond! After impressing with two centuries in his debut series, he was taken to England in 1930 and immediately re-wrote the record books: 974 runs in the Tests (average 139) in seven innings with 334 at Leeds, 232 at the Oval and 254 at Lord's. The Lord's achievement was a ground record for 60 years till Gooch eclipsed it in 1990. Four years later, he scored 304 at Leeds again. In his 52 Tests, Bradman totalled 6,996 runs, an aggregate later outstripped by several batsmen, including Gavaskar (10,122 runs); but Gavaskar did appear in many more innings.

Clearly then, the Australian must rank as the most celebrated and consistent of all batsmen. He was belligerent, attractive to watch, an awesome sight when in full flow, a veritable scourge of even the best bowlers. Unorthodox in his technique and methods (by textbook standards), he dominated the scene with a singleness of purpose and an exciting range of strokes that made him a legend. He was also a shrewd captain and later, an elder statesman of cricket as a respected administrator.

The English cricket writer, David Frith, has said of him: "He was not only a great batsman, but an exceptional human being as well........ Though I am a Bradman worshipper, I think it is unfair to compare him with Gavaskar; and he doesn't consider himself in the same category as that of the Don. Nor does Gregg Chappell. Very wise thinking......... But had Bradman been up against the four West Indian quickies, he would have survived but his run rate would have been less. Gavaskar had to face all these boys and this is the thing which impresses me most.....Against a wide range of bowling he has prospered."

This is a relevant point and yet I am convinced that all truly great batsmen are able to adapt to the technical and psychological challenges of any era. So that Gavaskar himself may have coped adequately with the bodyline bowling of Larwood and Voce before the war. His dedication, sound technique, massive powers of concentration, would have helped him immensely in this onerous task, even with a battering in the process.

Both Bradman and Gavaskar possessed an insatiable appetite for runs. Their methods varied. The former plundered the bowling but basically Gavaskar for much of his career, was an accumulator and an improvisor of runs, in the manner of say Boycott or Barrington. But when the mood was on him and the adrenalin started flowing, he could unleash an exciting array of strokes that kept the scoreboard ticking merrily along. His 29th century at Delhi, his 90 at Ahmedabad, his 96 in his final Test versus Pakistan at Bangalore in 1987, his Caribbean initiative of 1971 all attest to this.

He could be dour and defensive at times, since India's hopes of good totals often rested on his able shoulders. But he was seldom unattractive to watch or 'dogged' in the manner of Yorkshire's Boycott. A technician, Sunil certainly was, but on occasion a destroyer of the best bowling. The Indian crowds idolized him and recognized him as the greatest batsman ever produced by India, with the possible exception of the legendary wizard, Ranjitsinjhi, who played all his cricket for Sussex and England. Gavaskar never relished the one-day games, though his later years demonstrated his adjustment to them; he abhorred its artificiality but he was a Test batsman par excellence.

Brian Crowley of South Africa makes an interesting point when he says very succinctly "Bradman (apart from Bodyline in 1932-33) did not have to contend with the seemingly inevitable battery of fast bowlers in every international team, a phenomenon which Gavaskar usually handled with great physical courage and aplomb......One of the finest players of fast bowling in the world, with 13 Test centuries against the West Indies, a high proportion of his 34 that confirms his ability."

Vijay Merchant in commenting on both batsmen, emphasizes that Bradman rarely faced the wrath of the new ball and Gavaskar did this in a time when "cricket ceased to be a game.....And standards of pace bowling and fielding have improved today just like that of the athletes."

C.K. Harridas has stated relevantly: "Bradman was a child of his times; Gavaskar a child of his. In Bradman's day cricket was still a game; in the latter's, it is mimic warfare and a commercial enterprise with no holds barred. Being an opener, the Indian had his limitations and constraints, which rules out flamboyance of strokeplay, the Don's hallmark before the war....... Both became senior statesmen of world cricket."

Sir Len Hutton, who admired Gavaskar's technique, rates him among the best of all times. Hutton says: "I have a feeling that if he had been born English or Australian, many of the better judges would have been tempted to bracket him with Bradman. Gavaskar is not as good as Bradman but very close, which automatically puts him in the very highest class of batsmen of all times.........Certainly Gavaskar has a model technique. If I were to recommend a schoolboy to copy a modern master, I would go for Gavaskar rather than Viv Richards."

It must be pointed out that Gavaskar had a more sensational start to his Test career than Bradman who scored 18 and 1 on his debut, was then dropped but came back to make his mark as a batting genius and the bane of all bowlers. Gavaskar totalled 774 in his first series, but thereafter struggled for a while; Bradman never had an unproductive Test series and even when Larwood curbed his prolific powers in 1932-33, his average was 56.

To crystallize the discussion: Bradman dwarfs Gavaskar in purely statistical terms; as he does everyone else, even Hobbs, Headley and Richards. Both were master batsmen, colossal performers, artists of their craft, pride of their countrymen. Cricket is indeed richer for their superlative achievements for they both have carved an indelible niche in the annals of the game. Both admire each other with great sincerity and Gavaskar smartly asserts that it is fatuous to make comparisons.

CHAPTER 7

Harvest Of Fulfilment

The greatest satisfaction is in the fact that I played for India and that I achieved a few things in cricket as an Indian. I am proud of that fact.

Sunil Gavaskar

Consequently I rejoice, having to construct something upon which to rejoice.

T.S. Eliot: Ash Wednesday (1930)

Though India had achieved a memorable victory over the mighty West Indies in the final of the 1983 World Cup and though Gavaskar himself had enjoyed a successful series against Clive Lloyd's team which toured India in 1983-84, scoring more than 500 Test runs, India's cricket experienced a decline and the heady euphoria of the World Cup achievement had quickly faded with the 3-0 revenge triumph for the visitors.

Gavaskar has described all this in his third cricket book "Runs 'n Ruins" which was written around this time. He sadly contrasted his own batting form with the collective failure of the team, stating that the magnificent edifice of June 1983 now lay in ruins. In his "History of Indian Cricket" Mihir Bose remarks that the immediate future "brought more heartache for Gavaskar and Indian cricket. A wretched tug-of-war for the captaincy dominated the game." There was indeed a reversal of the captaincy and interpretations of its implications and consequences were diverse, sometimes informed but at most times inconsequential and absurd.

The season of 1984-85 began with the visit of an Australian team to mark and celebrate 50 years of the Ranji Trophy Tournament. No Tests were played; only four one-day internationals, three of which Australia won comfortably. Gavaskar was now back as captain for the tour of Pakistan in October 1984. The Tests at Lahore and Faisalabad were both drawn, but he was bitter about the standard of umpiring, particularly that of Shakoor Rana whom he openly accused of hometown bias at Lahore. A high scoring draw followed at Faisalabad (India 500, Pakistan 674 for 6 dec) but when the tragic news came of the assassination of Indira Ghandi, the rest of the tour was abandoned.

Soon after came an England visit to India which had seemed doubtful for a while in a climate of political violence. Eventually it was resolved that the scheduled 5-Test series continue as planned. India won the opening clash at Bombay by eight wickets, largely due to centuries by Shastri and keeper Kirmani in a total of 465 for 8 declared, while only Mike Gatting (136) played Sivaramakrishnan's (12 wickets in the match) legbreaks with any degree of assurance. But at Delhi, England levelled the series, despite Gavaskar's fighting 65 in the second innings. The visitors won by eight wickets, with their spinners Edmonds and Pocock bowling effectively. At Calcutta in the third Test, Gavaskar made his 88th successive Test appearance but failed with the bat in a drawn match where Azharuddin and Shastri scored hundreds. This was not a lucrative series for Gavaskar and England wrapped up the series 2-1 with a nine wicket win at Madras where Neil Foster claimed 11 wickets for 163 and both Gatting and Fowler made double centuries in a mammoth England total of 652 for 7 declared. India led on first innings in the final match at Kanpur where Azharuddin created history by scoring a century in each of his first three Tests, clearly a batsman with a bright future. David Gower's side returned home victorious and Gavaskar did not escape the censure of the vitriolic press, nor did the swashbuckling Kapil Dev for irresponsible batting at Delhi. Gavaskar had tried hard to square the series at Kanpur but the pitch was slow and England held on.

The writer Mihir Bose states "the press and the public, feeding on each other, had made Indian cricket a pressure-cooker and Gavaskar was being singed by the heat." His batting in the series was dismal (average 17.5) with only one innings above 50. He was led to critically study video replays of his batting in an effort to rectify his technique which seemed to have gone awry.

Yet just ahead lay a major triumph for him in the Benson and Hedges World Championship held in Australia. Here against all pre-tournament forecasts, India defeated all comers in splendid style, with Gavaskar and Shastri the deserving heroes of the tour.

The excitement of winning the Benson and Hedges was so overwhelming that the players surrounded Gavaskar and drenched him with champagne. Don Moraes relates that this act was not only one of affection "but a sort of awe." It was felt that Gavaskar's leadership and shrewdness were largely responsible for India's triumph. Mihir Bose sympathetically viewed Gavaskar's performance away from home as confident; free from the shackles of criticism and press hysteria.

It was in this climate that he was able to think with a sense of assurance and be more communicative with his players. On such a high note Gavaskar with his characteristic sense of timing gave up the captaincy and decided to represent India as a player until retirement.

In August 1985, India visited Sri Lanka for a short series, with Kapil Dev, not Gavaskar, at the helm. The latter batted in the middle order at number 5 or 6, and made two scores over 50. After a drawn match, India surprisingly lost to their hosts in the second Test by 149 runs and had to settle for the better of a drawn affair at Kandy.

In December of the same year, India again toured Australia for a 3-Test series. At Adelaide Gavaskar slammed an unbeaten 166 on a bland, benign pitch where India reached 520 in response to Australia's 381. For the Australians, Boon and Ritchie both got centuries. It was also in this match that Kapil

Dev's feat of 8 wickets for 106 mesmerized the Australian side. Gavaskar's 166 was a monumental effort. It revealed his remarkable powers of concentration and dedication. There were some disturbing moments against the lifting delivery but he batted with "supreme judgement and concentration." The innings has been described as "an object lesson to youngsters who were watching the match as well as the opposing Australian batsmen." This incidentally was Sunil's 31st Test hundred and his first since his double century versus the West Indies at Madras in December 1983. At this time he had also scored 9000 runs in Test cricket.

India were well-placed to win at Melbourne with fine spin bowling by Shastri who was ably supported by Yadav, but some dubious tactics by Kapil Dev let Australia off the hook on the final day.

A brilliant innings of 172 by Gavaskar, now timing the ball well again, paced India to 600 for 4 declared at Sydney, the Aussie attack taking a hammering from Srikkanth, Gavaskar and Mohinder Amarnath. The match petered out into a draw after glimpses of an Indian win. So Kapil Dev, after 20 Tests as skipper, had yet to win a Test. Gavaskar scored 352 runs (av 117) in this series and was back to his normal consistency after a frustrating run-drought. Having relinquished the captaincy in 1985, he seemed at peace with himself again, and he once more took upon himself the responsibility of opening the Indian's innings.

In the early summer of 1986, India toured England again, once more with Kapil Dev optimistically at the helm. England had just returned from a disastrous tour of the Caribbean where for the second time they had suffered a 5-0 humiliation versus the triumphant West Indies. Perhaps because of this, India's hopes soared and indeed they won the Lord's Test by five wickets and the match at Headingly, Leeds by 279 runs. Gavaskar played a moderate role in these victories and Dilip Vengsarkar performed creditably. At Leeds, England were routed for totals of 102 and 128, Binny and Maninder Singh the chief destroyers of the home team.

Both teams scored 390 in the Edgbaston game, where Gavaskar celebrated his 115th Test appearance, scoring a vital 54 in the second innings but the match was drawn giving India victory in the series for only the second time on English soil. This tour proved to be the final one Sunil made to England as a player.

Back home in triumph, India now prepared for a tough series with Allan Border's visiting team, comprising players of the calibre of Boon, Dean Jones, Steve Waugh, McDermott and Bruce Reid. At Madras in the first Test, the teams battled to only the second ever tied match in Test cricket history, emulating the Brisbane tie of 1960 between the Aussies and Worrell's West Indian team. The date was September 22, 1986 and the scores in this historic affair were Australia 574 for 7 declared, and 170 for 5 declared; India 397 and 347. It was a thrilling game watched by thousands.

Boon, Jones and Kapil Dev hit hundreds, while Gavaskar made a superb and invaluable 90 in the crucial denouement of the match. But for his score, India may have lost; as it was, dogged India batting took them within sight of an improbable victory before Maninder Singh fell LBW to Greg Matthews with the score level.

Rain ruined the second Test at Delhi and in the last clash at Bombay, Gavaskar's 103 and Vengsarkar's 164 not out gave India the better of a drawn match. It was Sunil's 33rd Test century and his eighth against Australia.

Gavaskar was again in prolific form when Sri Lanka led by Duleep Mendis, toured India in December, 1986. In a high scoring game at Kanpur, he achieved the last of his 34 Test centuries with an attractive display of 176. Centuries from Gavaskar, Azharuddin and Kapil Dev contributed to India's highest ever total in Test cricket: 676 for 7 declared. This was in reply to Sri Lanka's creditable 420. And in the following Test at Nagpur, Gavaskar contributed 74 (batting at No. 5) to a healthy Indian total of 451 for 6 declared. The home team won by an innings, with the left arm spin of Maninder Singh routing Sri Lanka for 204 and 141.

In the final match at Cuttack, the 60th Test venue, India again won by an innings. Gavaskar made only 5, but a century by Vengsarkar and fine spin bowling sealed the issue.

Sunil Gavaskar played his last Test series against his country's arch-rivals Pakistan in February, 1987. For the record, his scores in four matches were 91, 0, 24, 63, 21 and 96. He 'missed' the second Test at Calcutta, a decision which aroused disturbing reactions for it was felt that he boycotted it because of unruly crowd's personal abuse of himself and his wife Pammi.

The first four Tests were drawn - traditional wars of attrition between these two countries - with neither captains Imran Khan nor Kapil Dev showing much enterprise.

It was basically a high scoring series; but the final clash at Bangalore was a bowler's match. Pakistan made 116 and 249 while India scored 145 and 204. Gavaskar's 96 in the second innings was a brilliant knock "a supreme exhibition of temperament and technique," in the words of renowned statistician Bill Frindall.

Kapil Dev remarked that "it was one of the finest knocks I've ever seen." The Pakistan skipper, Imran Khan, reflected "I think it compares favourably with the double hundred notched up at the Oval." After the match, Imran remarked "It's about the best Gavaskar innings I've seen. It was so well calculated, well planned." On a turning pitch of uneven bounce, he demonstrated why he is regarded as one of the pantheon of great batsmen; sound in defence, discreet in his strokeplay and punishing the loose balls to the boundary. Mihir Bose summed up his display: "He showed all the qualities that made him a batting legend."

But for all this "superlative and superhuman effort from Sunil Gavaskar," declared Lokendra Partap Sahi, "16 runs separated the combatants." Sahi reports that when the Master's innings had ended, India's aspirations of winning the Test also ended. An extremely disappointed Gavaskar walked back to the pavilion only four short of his 35th Test century, but greeted with tremendous applause and ovation.

Gavaskar's gallant effort proved in vain, Pakistan winning by a mere 16 runs. It was felt that Gavaskar would announce his retirement from Test cricket after the Pakistan tour but he did play in the 1987 World Cup played in India and Pakistan, and later that year, in August, finally scored a superb century at Lord's which had earlier eluded him. He made a classic 188 for a Rest of the World team versus MCC at age 38. Then he announced his retirement.

Throughout Gavaskar's career his strong sense of nationalism was evident. His achievements transformed him into a national hero. But there was no need to assert his nationalism through cricketing supremacy; his varied achievements and successes meant that India was able to assert herself and compete at the highest level on the international scene. This ability to achieve and perform is very well recognized in the most powerful countries for Indians are key players in these countries.

Nationalism is deep-rooted in India. The Indian, through his spiritually fertile inheritance is born with a deep sense of nationalism and he lives it; and this, Gavaskar has always shown in word and deed. In 1971 he was the main force in transforming India into a major force in world cricket. His career and the talent which began to proliferate from the seventies (the consistent spin quartet with able replacements, the arrival of Kapil Dev, the talents of Vengsarkar, Azharuddin, Shastri, Srikkanth, Sandeep Patil, Mohinder Amarnath, Tendulkar and Vinod Kambli) signify the new Indian emerging, not the Indian character which has been shrouded in docility. Its assertion is evident in the contribution of science and technology and the deep philosophical school of thought with its spiritual significance which has been attracting western philosophers and thinkers. Gavaskar's presence, whether he recognizes it or not, has gone beyond the limits of cricket and has to be viewed in the broader perspective of India's presence on the international scene.

When Gavaskar speaks of his 'Indianness' he rejoices in it and the fulfiling achievements gained for India. After his grand deeds at Delhi and Madras against the West Indies in 1983, he seemed destined to tread the paths of glory. It seemed that he was truly earmarked for greatness. His career continued to flourish despite some inconsistent parts. The total picture during the twilight of his career reveals achievement not only for himself but for his country. The special events which climaxed his career were his one-day century at Nagpur, his ten thousand runs record, his Benson and Hedges triumph and his rhythmical swansong at Lord's in which he exhibited perfection of technique. At his retirement here at 38, it was a true triumph of his craft, of spirit and heroism.

It was at Ahmedabad that the 10,000th run was posted. In Steven Lynch's analysis of Gavaskar's 10,000 Test runs he states *"Just after tea on March 7, the third day of the drawn fourth Test match against Pakistan at Ahmedabad, India's Little Master, Sunil Manohar Gavaskar, cut a ball from offspinner Ijaz Faqih through the slips for two, taking him past a career total of 10,000 runs in Test cricket. Gavaskar, 37, was batting in his 124th match and 212th innings, both of which are Test records, as of course, is his run aggregate. He has scored more Test centuries and fifties than any other player."*

On reaching his 10,000 runs record, in his prevailing modesty, he remarked "I never expected to score 10,000. I would have been pleased with 1,000. Actually, its 9,000 runs too many." This was the Gavaskar, who on entry to Test cricket, was only eager not to make a fool of himself. His expectations were modest and practical. This is the same Gavaskar who was happy to say "I think batsmen like Border, Miandad, Gower and Richards have a good chance to overtake me. But it is always nice to be the first. After all, a lot of people have climbed Everest, but the ones I remember most are Hillary and Tenzing."

Gavaskar had also shown no keen interest in one-day performances. But later in his career, there was greater sureness of touch and he performed creditably. One of the significant achievements in this type of cricket (apart from his Benson and Hedges triumphant performance, particularly as captain) was his only century of 103 not out against New Zealand at Nagpur.

Henry Blofield describes the innings as "one of a lifetime, both for Gavaskar himself and those who saw it," and exclaims that it was "the most refined and cultured form of destruction" he had ever seen. Blofield continues "At Lord's he was the perfectionist Test match opener; at Nagpur he was the perfect one-day batsman."

The innings revealed character; it exuded grace and elegance. It was an exhibition in which concentration and will power assisted in the pursuit of excellence. It was an innings made memorable through the purity of strokes and a sense of resilience which overcame the burdens of exhaustion and the high fever he suffered.

Gavaskar's achievements were varied and it is difficult to put them in order of merit though his record number of centuries and his 10,000 runs record will always be popularly acknowledged. But at the end of his career his conquest at Lord's will linger forever in the memory.

It was in that MCC Bicentenary celebration in 1987 at Lord's, the commemoration of 200 years of cricket, Gavaskar was selected to play for the Rest of the World against an MCC XI. The event has been popularly deemed as successful and entertaining. It brought together some of the most brilliant and conspicuous talent from various cricketing countries. In Trevor Bailey's words "There was assembled at Lord's probably the finest collection of cricketers to take part in the game." But three others of world class stature, Martin Crowe and Ian Botham through injury, and Richards of his own choice, missed this match.

The wicket was a batsman's paradise and certainly most of them made capital of it against bowling of a high calibre and great skill. Among the accumulators, the four notable G's: Gooch, Gatting, Greenidge and Gavaskar all exhibited their talent to the delight of the cricketing audience. But most remarkable of all was the grand innings played by Gavaskar. It was his first and only century at Lord's and by virtue of its quality was recognized as the best innings of the match. For this he was named Batsman of the match. In all his cricketing years a three figure score had eluded him at Lord's. Now just before retirement he performed what was called an admirable feat achieved with brilliance, skill and sound technique. During his innings he demonstrated his incomparable technical perfection and artistry when confronted with the speed of Marshall, the movement of Hadlee and the flight of Shastri. Martin Jenkins remarked that "only the continuing pace and hostility of Marshall tested the speed of Gavaskar's eyes and feet." In an article entitled "Four Days of Heaven" Jenkins describes his innings:

"With lovely, orthodox grace he made his first century at Lord's in his last first-class match before retiring as the first man to make 10,000 Test runs. No one has demonstrated better, that to bat effectively, whether like Gavaskar you are 5ft 4.75ins, or a giant like his old adversary Greig, the most important thing is to have your head over the ball as you play. No one knows the smell of a cricket ball better than Gavaskar."

His innings of 188, described by David McMahon as a "nugget of memorable perfection" included 23 fours and was terminated by his own countryman, student and friend, Ravi Shastri, who, through his clever flight, induced Gavaskar to offer a return catch.

The Rest of the World replied with 420 for 7 declared in response to the MCC's first innings of 455 for 5. On their second attempt the MCC accumulated 318 for 6 and gave the Rest of the World 353 to chase for victory. No positive conclusion was reached because of heavy torrents which marred an otherwise splendid game in fine weather. But before the gathering clouds put an end to play, Gavaskar had his second stint at the crease which proved to be an anti-climax. McMahon in memorable language describes Gavaskar's exit, "Gavaskar, having fulfiled what was expected of him, went Bradmanlike - without scoring in his final innings - confounded by the cricketing gods and bowled by Malcolm Marshall."

It is compelling to include in this piece the descriptions which accompanied his majestic display. John Woodcock writing in the "Times" declared that "it was made with such touch and assurance, indeed such mastery as to make his retirement at the age of 38 seem altogether premature."

R. Mohan in describing the ovation as he returned to the pavilion through the passageway, on to the dressing room, writes "a sea of humanity parted just sufficiently for the great man to pass. The applause was deafening, the back-patting frightening and the reception overwhelming," and he continues by singling it out as "an innings representative of the arts and graces of purist batsmanship."

Ted Dexter reporting in the "Sunday Mirror" scrolled "Sunil Gavaskar turned MCC's showpiece into a wonderful retirement party."

Bill Frindall in the "Mail" on Sunday describes it as an innings of character and near technical perfection. It was an innings studded with numerous wristy strokes of the purest pedigree," and Val Gibson in the "Sunday Express" relates "Gavaskar, surely the greatest opening batsman in the history of the game, delayed announcing his retirement from Test cricket to make sure he got the chance to achieve his last cricketing ambition."

If Raj Singh Dungarpur were to respond to Gibson's comment, he would tell you that Gavaskar was a "Master of Timing" both at the crease and beyond it. And this innings surely was one of his more fulfiling ones.

So he went out of the game with an appropriate flourish which quite suited his stature. And though Gavaskar was never seen in action again, his "influence and presence" in Indian cricket lives on, fuelled by his contribution with the pen, his charisma as an elder statesman and the abiding memories of his ardent admirers who saw him in the flesh, not long ago, in his halcyon days at the crease, delighting a multitude with the quality of his craft.

CHAPTER 8

Towards Perfecting His Craft

The excellence of every art is its intensity.
John Keats

T he knowledgeable and insightful critics of the game have seen in Gavaskar a total personal commitment to an ideal, an aspiration to stylistic form unique and consistent; in essence, a technique in batting skill and craft as the cornerstone of his sporting existence. With him there was an engagement with the game and he played it with a fascination that transcended ordinary limits, at all times dedicated to the demanding requirements of his technique.

For Gavaskar, technical perfection was achieved not only through physical dexterity but intellectual contemplation. In fact, to a great extent the more enhancing and stylistic features of the game, its technique, elegance, finesse in stroke-making make demands on the intellect, the challenges of concentration and application. It does not require the complexity of thought that informs an intellectual discipline but judgement and shrewdness, a grasp of the variables of a bowling attack, an astuteness and play of mind fused with physical attributes of dexterity, nimbleness and artistry, all intellectual and physical, which are the qualities that make a gifted craftsman at the wicket. In perfecting his technique, Gavaskar was thought and skill oriented, employing an understanding of the process of batting and adjusting to the varying situations which he encountered, especially as an opener. His concentration was intense, his application demonstrated method, thought coupled with a spirit of enthusiasm on most occasions at the crease. Some of his finest innings revealed the man who combined skill and spirit to produce batting of expert technical standard.

At a very tender age a strong competitive spirit was evident. There was that passion for continuous hours of batting without indication of lack of interest or boredom or tiredness. It was concentration and application unique for a child. And as he grew up he nurtured an intense, unwavering passionate interest in the game which he looked at with a keenness of observation.

During his early years his batting style or technique was influenced by his father, Manohar, who watched him regularly and advised him, thereby helping him to eliminate flaws in his technique. His uncle, Madhav Mantri, was also instrumental in inculcating a great measure of discipline in his approach to the game. Mantri advised him strongly never to give his wicket away recklessly in spite of his high scores. At a coaching camp in Hyderabad organized for schoolboys under the supervision of T.S. Worthington, an English coach, he was initiated into the 'finer points of the game'. Sunil was taught never to play chest-open while facing the bowler and he learnt of the importance of playing side-on. This to him was the greatest single contributing factor in his career.

During his early years as a schoolboy cricketer his stance was faulty. He gripped his bat so tight and held it at an angle that he was most likely to edge the ball to the slips than hit it out of the ground. It was Kamal Bhandarkar, a former Maharastra player, who noticed it and taught him the proper grip. He recalled that during play when in difficulty he remembered Kamal's advice and checked his grip. Dadar Union Club's fraternity with Mantri and V.S. Patil among others all played a significant role in the development of his craft and technique. Such was his eye for detail that he was captivated by Conrad Hunte's backlift, high and straight, together with his movement of his front foot to the line of the ball.

As Gavaskar developed he paid more attention to the trappings which go with the performance........ bat, gloves, head gear, skull-cap. Because of his height and his particular stance he used a blade 3/4 of an inch longer than the standard size. His leg-guards were moulded and he was the only successful player who kept using them. To meet the demands of pace, since he never wore a helmet, he developed a special skull-cap which really only protected his temple. His proneness to injury on the finger made him devise a "double sausage roll" on top of the overflap of his second and third fingers. This device is impact resistant; it reduces the impact of the ball or absorbs shock easily by distributing its force. This glove is now popularly used. This meticulous attention to detail was integral in his approach to his craft. It reflected the seriousness with which he considered its part in the game.

In this specialty of batting there was care, seriousness and obvious willingness to perform, a readiness for the challenge, not a routine or pedestrian application to the craft. Knowledge of the variety of bowling styles was one of the main requisites in his approach to countering the attack. There was a perceptive mind at work in his assessment of the opponents' strengths and weaknesses. To perform at the highest level with quality and distinction meant a constant evaluation of the game and its varying demands. What marked him out above the others was his unfailing ability to concentrate, a demanding mental exercise. He recalls that:

"....... when it came to a fast bowler, I was very keen to know what he did, whether he brought the ball back in, whether he was good at bowling a yorker, whether he was good at bowling the short one, whether his short ball was a surprise, much quicker than normal deliveries."

The attention to such significant details as the bowler's technique and guile always kept him alert and conscious of the innings ahead. For instance, the spin bowler always aroused his curiosity and taxed his mental readiness:

"did he flight? did he tire?" were questions which preoccupied him. In his first series in the West Indies he encountered Lance Gibbs, the record holder at that time for the highest number of Test wickets. Lance would take one minute and a half to complete an over. It was this kind of rhythm that Gavaskar observed. In response when he took time to take strike, Lance would be upset because this counter-approach disturbed Lance's rhythm. Gavaskar's ploy was effective for it unnerved Lance and this to him was "a psychological game and you want to get the upper hand."

It is interesting to note that his dressing room preparation had assumed an 'air of a ritual'. In warm climates he would take about fifteen minutes and about twenty minutes in cold countries before he was prepared for the crease. This time was spent jogging on the balls of his feet, imaginary strokes off the front and back foot, placing his protective box, securing his pads properly to his feet, making certain of his thigh and arm guards, and finally putting on his batting gloves. During the course of dressing he would be shadow practising and before he left the pavilion he never forgot to put on his floppy sun-hat. Everything was done meticulously.

It is fair to conclude that his attention to the rudiments and fundamentals of his craft such as his preparation and his emphasis on correctness of technique to suit diverse conditions, contributed to making him one of the most prolific opening batsmen of all times. At times one would think he was striving like the artist for clarity and precision. In him it was the pursuit of excellence in his attempt to be in control, to avoid the bowler gaining even intermittent control of the situation.

His irrepressible mood in the Caribbean and the nature of his innings indicated the shaping and development of a craftsman, not a mere batsman. As some of his spectacular innings grew in confidence in the Caribbean you could have noticed the actual and deliberate moulding and shaping of the innings, a compactness and structural wholeness of form, free from fragmentation, but full of concentration and application. And as he developed and matured there was the same kind of tightness, compactness against adverse conditions, particularly at Worcester in 1974, and Old Trafford in '71 and '74.

In adverse conditions where inclement weather proved

devastating there was always the need to improvise, to use the benefit of knowledge and technique to counter such attacks. Sunil always remembers during his formative years in Test cricket, that villainous wicket at Old Trafford where he scored 57 and has recognized it as his best innings in Test cricket. It seemed one of the most challenging that he experienced. The bowlers in exploiting the conditions made the ball fly past. With his technique he was able to keep the ball down. Every time it lifted he would drop his wrists and let it pass or if it did come in, he would be right behind it to be able to put it down. His intention in the circumstances, was to prevent it "from flying off the edge or its cocking up in the air."

It is appropriate to recall Vijay Merchant's comment on Gavaskar's score of 205 against West Indies at Wankhede Stadium. Merchant felt it was his best innings up to that time. It was a damp pitch and the ball was swinging. For Merchant, Sunil proved beyond doubt that he could play fast bowling on a damp pitch as well. It was a great tribute to hear Merchant, one of the finest technicians of India's batting, appeal to all budding cricketers to observe Sunil's batting, "for there cannot be a better model for anybody wanting to learn the art of batsmanship." This thought was articulated by Sir Len Hutton later during Gavaskar's career.

The limit of his height did not afford him the measure of flexibility that would have facilitated him in responding aggressively and countering the attack as he wished. The pull shot was not among his repertoire because of his height and this impeded his counter-attack. He expressed great admiration for Martin Crowe's expertise and recognized Viv Richards as a tremendous puller. If affected by bowling which was short of a length, the pull shot enabled batsmen to break the shackles and come to terms with the attack.

Though impressed by his batting technique and his penchant for massive scores, critics often referred to his tendency to be a defensive player without flair and flamboyance. His style, they thought, was not of the cavalier. But it must be said that the many who followed his Test career from its inception would clearly assert that there was the attacking rhythm and flair in his Caribbean innings of 1971. This style was subdued when the pressure of his personal pursuit at the wicket was subordinated in the interest of the team. He certainly had to support the innings with his presence as almost a "sheet anchor". This was his dilemma; he had to lend stability to the innings in the majority of times and this detracted from his individual style. In the process he may not have played all the delightful strokes as freely and as much as people liked. One could say that he was literally forced into that role. Vijay Merchant in a lucid statement said that Sunil "started as a stroke player, but later went into a shell no doubt realizing how much responsibility rested on his shoulders in the light of India's frail batting."

It must be remembered that during the '70's he decided to eliminate the hook shot. It was too risky to chance a valuable innings with such a seemingly cavalier shot. Ian Botham while observing his exceptional quickness of feet when the bowler drops short of length, also knew that bumpers to Sunil was wasted ammunition because he would "weave and bob out of range so nimbly." Later in 1983 after his 29th Test century he recalled how he eliminated the hook shot.

"I used to hook uppishly and the chances were high I could lose my wicket. In a nutshell it was not a percentage shot, in the sense, the four runs could put me in grave peril, so it was not worth it. Then again you have to admit I was under a lot of pressure, all these years and since I do not have many days before me, it's time I should enjoy my batting. What better satisfaction can one get than a scintillating innings, studded with hits to the boundary. I try to play as many shots as possible, even if it means starting right from the first ball of the day. I am really enjoying my batting today and wish to continue that way."

Here is an expression of a player who was capable of executing the finest array of strokes but who through commitment to his team, subdued his natural style. He now re-shaped it as the circumstances required. This he demonstrated during his 29th century and his 90 at Ahmedabad. According to his wife Marshneil these were memorable innings, different from what he normally played. She noted about these innings in particular: "Perhaps" she says "I got a vicarious kick out of these knocks after what people have been saying all these years about Sunil being a very defensive player."

Marshneil's contention does reveal a balanced judgement and practical view of the state of his batting:

"On the one side people have attacked him for being unpatriotic when he was to join Kerry Packer, and on the other side when he stood for hours like a strokeless wonder, trying to hold the side together for the sake of the country, people have said he is a bore. That he has no strokes of his own. These innings have at least proved that he wanted to play strokes all the time, and would have perhaps played them better when he was younger, had it not been for the fact that he had always put his side's interest before his and sacrificed his natural stroke-making."

Vasu Paranjpe, who advised him on a change of technique to meet the demands of the situation exclaimed:

"His stroke-studded innings of a century at Delhi and 90 at Ahmedabad must go down as two of the best innings he has ever played in his glittering career!"

It is interesting to view his technique and batting prowess in the light of what some of the most knowledgeable people, (senior and former players and contemporaries) have articulated.

Mike Brearley, one of England's finest captains, who played against Gavaskar has expressed admiration for him as the best opening batsmen he has seen in Test matches, better than Gordon Greenidge or Geoff Boycott. Brearley's alertness to Gavaskar's technique is quoted here:

"He has perfect technique, good balance and is almost never

rattled or made to look ungainly. Where he has the edge over Boycott is that he hardly ever allows the half volley to go unpunished and will hit it for four in most cases. He is remarkably good against short-pitched bowling for a man of his height and is able to sway or duck out of harm's way with the greatest ease and elegance. He can also hook but it is not his strongest point."

In describing Gavaskar as "simply the best opening batsman in the world," Fred Truman, one of England's most effective fast bowlers of the 50's and 60's, emphasizes:
"Sunny's strength is his compactness. He is small but very quick and he seems to have so much time to play the ball. Like all great players he has a sound defence, but can turn just as smoothly to attack the minute he senses the slightest weakness in the bowler. Certainly he never lets his opponent dominate and is very difficult to get out of position."

The endless stream of comparison continues between Boycott and Gavaskar, and Truman recognizes "Sunny is better than Geoff Boycott. Though possessing a good defence, is limited as a one-pace player, while Sunil has the ability to move into a higher gear whenever it suits him." However, Truman feels that Len Hutton with his array of strokes and elegance was a greater batsman than Sunil. Bishen Bedi sees him as an accumulator of runs, not a destroyer of bowling. Frank Keating, a columnist with the London Guardian, feels that Sunil does nothing flamboyant but gets runs. Keating is however impressed with his footwork as "almost an artform, never faulted". But West Indian veterans are more impressed. Lloyd thinks he had every stroke in the book. Sobers rates him as the best during his time and Kanhai emphasizes that "it is wrong to say that he does not have strokes. He has all of them. Off the front foot and back foot; on the onside and offside. And he is very, very competent playing each of them."

Though conscious of his ability to play a diverse assortment of strokes, Sunil very modestly felt that he had not mastered a few of them. He asserted that he never mastered the hook stroke; his height denied him the pull shot; there was no late cut in his range and he regretted his inability to master the classic cover drive. Of this he said:

"I generally slice my cover drive in a pendulum like swing from squarish deep fine and finishing with the full face of the bat towards cover, like Hammond or Hazare."

Gavaskar's career prospered in an era of pace. Though he was effective against spin and medium pace, his competence against pace was always noted. It was his ability to withstand the ferocity of pace so consistently that earned him his gallantry and glory on the international scene. It was in his very first Test appearance that he was pitted against the Caribbean pace, though it might not have had the usual venom but later as he played he encountered the full blast from every cricketing country. As in Shakespeare's "Henry V" it was like the" full blast of war". For the seventies was the era when the full blast expressed itself either in three or four pronged attacks. The Australians started the reign of terror when they treated Clive Lloyd's West Indians to its bitter taste concluding in a demoralizing 5-1 defeat. It was Thomson's and Lillee's devastating spells which left them shell-shocked and dispirited. From then on the West Indies, garnering their forces found they were capable of dominating the show, though the Australians continued to use their weaponry to advantage. With venomous express attacks there were memories of the bodyline series between England and Australia. Now in the seventies with the catalogue of injuries listed on each side, whether England, Australia, West Indies or India, it brought to the game an ugly appearance. It was not bodyline repeated but in its menacing attack it could easily have been labelled 'bloodyline'. The injuries, if known fully to the global cricketing audience would terrify and would certainly lead the scholars to think they were at some time or the other, looking at some parts of Greek tragedy. In Shakespearian language, the bowlers would "summon up their spirits, disguise fair nature in hard favoured rage and lend the eye a terrible aspect." The eyes were made to "pry through the portage of the head like a brass canon." The sinews would stiffen and the spirit would be bent to his full height.

It was this type of warfare, this intimidatory bowling that left the English devastated. It was this type of bowling which was served up to Sunil in the 1976 West Indian tour; a foretaste of the venom the West Indians would unleash on him in later years, both at home and abroad. His consistency and obduracy earned him their unwilling respect. And there were others on his team, Mohinder Amarnath, Vengsarkar, Srikkanth and Vishwanath who also gallantly faced the unrelenting pace attack.

Those who studied Sunil's response saw a 'correctness of technique'. Gopal Bhose recalls:

"Starting from the stance, with the body evenly balanced; with the weight evenly distributed on both feet and on the heels in particular, this being particularly evident as his toes kept clear off the ground." Bhose continues "He is fairly upright, that is as much as his height allows him to, but the moment preceding the delivery of the ball, Sunil goes into a noticeable crouch, bending from the knees and waist and the bat raised to stump level, which makes him such a glorious driver of the ball, hitting right through it." This is different from Boycott who is restricted by his top-bottom grip and is contented to merely push through the shot.

Vijay Hazare, as observant as Bhose, noticed Sunil's "relaxed, controlled stance, always in perfect position to execute a flowing stroke or a defensive prod. While executing strokes, his bat and pad are close together, not allowing even a streak of sunlight to pierce them. When he plays square of the wicket, his head and shoulders are always in line, feet firmly placed in line of the delivery ensuring that the stumps are covered."

Hazare also recalls Sunil's searching questions about his technique and that he was always thinking of the game. Imran Khan felt that he was "the most compact player he ever bowled to, playing near to his body with a straight bat and with the ability to make quick adjustments......... a great asset for an opening batsman against the moving ball." In describing Sunil as the finest opening batsman he ever bowled against, Bob Willis saw his technique as very much from the textbook, different from Viv Richards who was an instinctive and unorthodox player. Willis found that Sunil was very expert at playing the rising ball and with his footwork and superb balance he knew where the off-stumps were.

Simon Wilde in his "Letting Rip" details the atrocities of fast bowling in a very interesting and readable exposé. The devastation of pace abridged the career of some, others took their knocks with fortitude and the more courageous and skilful reacted positively, and these were few. If Turner and Zaheer deliberately escaped the firing line, David Steele, Derek Randall and Rick Darling were a few who demonstrated bravery and courage. In particular the bouncer was the weapon which they either hooked or played in defence. Tony Greig waged a psychological war to stifle the bowler's aggression but this was not very effective; Mohinder Amarnath for a period exuded confidence; Viv Richards and his colleagues though at times felt the pressure, were not to be humiliated again and courageously met the attack. But every batsman however successful against pace was apprehensive in the face of a menacing attack.

How did Sunil fare? He had begun his career in an aggressive mood, even defying use of head gear. As he progressed he eliminated the hook shot since it was too risky and his restraint was necessary for India's salvation. Defence became his forte and his defiance of bowling attacks was cause for concern. The West Indians in particular, were determined to penetrate his armour, "to find chinks in it" for he had played resolutely and with a considerable amount of freedom against them. Their campaign began in 1976, particularly at Sabina. He was enjoying a good series and even though at Sabina he experienced difficulty with the ball rising to the batsman's chin, he defied the attack with a solid 66 while all his colleagues through injury or fear surrendered to the barrage. Though the bowling was attacking, particularly Marshall, going around the wicket, it was as if by instinct, according to Shekhar Gupta, that he seemed to avoid the fast rising ball. He did it as if, says the Pakistani commentator, Iftikhar Ahmed, it were an "art perfected into a science."

In Skekhar Gupta's analysis of his batting he realized that constant video study was done in an attempt to serve him the right diet so he would succumb. Alan Davidson recommended persistent short pitched stuff. And it appeared in the early eighties that his early technique of fending off the fast rising ball and his judgement of the ball leaving the off-stump which he had mastered incomparably, were no longer part of his expertise. He seemed to be losing that gift. It was a matter of sparring at outgoing ones or jabbing at the short ones going to his chin. Gupta contends that he developed the suicidal shuffle towards the off-stump which made his leg-stump vulnerable. Gavaskar himself confessed that "I sort of did not know where my off-stump was."

Ashis Ray felt that Gavaskar's surfeit of Test cricket accounted for his apparent decline. He felt that it was the confrontation of too much quick bowling and its constant prevalence which caused 'chinks' in his concentration. Ray, in examining the West Indian position, saw the ploy to bowl Marshall from around the wicket and train a lethal attack on the body. And as Gavaskar was not hooking he fell in the trap. It signalled that he could no longer with ease get into line or away from the line of the fastest balls. Nor was there mental sturdiness to wear out the pressure of the bouncers.

Critics began to see a different Gavaskar, one who they felt was losing the reflexes he was so proud of. Ray reports that in 1983, on a lively pitch at Port of Spain during the first innings Sunil was not in line to Holding's kicking delivery. Against Marshall in the second innings he experienced a most awkward body attack. He did not succumb but left his off-side technique badly exposed so that he was driving too early or not getting into position.

With only a century in Guyana it was felt that he did not negotiate the pace effectively on Kensington's bouncing pitch or even in Antigua. Sunil felt that some good deliveries accounted for his dismissals on quite a few occasions. In the World Cup he was striking the ball too early or flirting with deliveries outside the off-stump. This period of inconsistency followed him at Kanpur where he failed against the West Indies on both occasions at the wicket.

Gavaskar understood his discomfort. He knew his reflexes were not getting sharper and there was an abundance of cricket. His mind had been jaded. Before this he had been technically correct and even by instinct was able to handle the short balls. In 1983 he decided to wear the skull cap which was lighter than the helmet and less cumbersome. With this protective gear which protected his temple he re-introduced the hook shot as part of his determination to go on the aggressive. It must be remembered that he failed in the Caribbean in 1983 and felt that containment of the pacers was not the solution at this stage. Also he realized that with experience there were those in the team who could give a good account of themselves so it left him with an option to, as he said after his 29th century, "enjoy my cricket".

It must be mentioned that though he was apprehensive about the kind of pace directed at him, he was never really hit or injured and unlike many of his colleagues he never appeared to be afraid. Counter attack now became part of his technique. After Kanpur's failure he took the attack to the bowlers in Delhi during the second Test. As Marshall bowled his bouncers he countered by hooking successfully. His 50 came in 37 balls, his hundred in 94 balls. This he followed at Ahmedabad facing 120 balls and making 90 runs. This was then followed by failure in 5 innings but in typical Gavaskar style he re-emerged hitting Marshall for fours off his first three deliveries and went on to an unbeaten 236. With the considerable amount of pace hurled at him, he found delight in his strokes which enhanced his image and deflated the bowlers.

In his attempt to break the shackles of defensive play, he demonstrated a technique fraught with embellishments and flamboyance and at times moments of inconsistency. His one-day cricket also began to exhibit flourishes and success. The very nature of the aggression invited risks. But when he realized that he was indulging in excesses he resorted to his essential defence.

Raj Singh Dungarpur speaks of one prime virtue that Gavaskar enjoyed: "In his mind he has always been the student, not the master. He overcame his trouble, perhaps even mental staleness and fatigue by a blend of judicious defence and authoritative offence and once again crowned himself to the unique position of being the best opening batsman of contemporary cricket."

And at the very end, his special technique did not fail him. His 96 in the final Test innings against Pakistan and eventually his swan song at Lord's are indicative of this. B.B. Mama describes his Lord's farewell innings as one of "flawless technique, absolute mastery of movement and co-ordination."

His rhythm, vitality, variety of stroke-play, use of foot-work against pace, approach to spin and his running between wickets (one of his great strengths) all indicated that at 38 he still possessed remarkable soundness of technique. His remarkable style reflected a fusion of thought and skill towards the perfection of his craft. This was most apparent in his farewell at Lord's. This concept of his art or craft is likened to Mathew Arnold's belief in poetry as "thought and art in one" and this to both of them is 'the glory, the eternal honour'.

CHAPTER 9

The Reluctant Captain

*The best of leaders are at times disillusioned
in the midst of adverse conditions.*

Anon

When Sunil Gavaskar, at the age of 29, was named as India's captain for the six Test series against the touring West Indies cricket team in November, 1978, his official appointment was viewed by reputable cricket critics, as well as the Indian public at large, as being in the eternal fitness of things.

It seemed to most followers of the game throughout the Commonwealth an inevitable step in his burgeoning cricket career, a natural development for which the celebrated Bombay batsman was earmarked ever since he made his dramatic entry on the international stage some eight years before on his first overseas tour to the Caribbean in 1971.

During his years of cricket before his appointment to the captaincy, he had brought dedication and discipline to the art of batsmanship, with an equable temperament for the big occasion, a sound technique and exciting strokeplay, which endeared him to Caribbean crowds. There were periods of disappointment, moderate successes, greater successes, fluctuations in his performances as he gained experience against different cricketing countries. As a team man he witnessed the demise of Wadekar, the recall of the Nawab of Pataudi Jr., and then the appointment of the turbaned Sikh, Bishen Bedi, the left-armed spinner, to the mantle of captaincy on a tour of New Zealand and the Caribbean in 1976.

A leg injury to Bedi on the eve of the first Test at Auckland gave Gavaskar an opportunity to lead India. He made a valid contribution to his team's eight wicket victory with scores

138

of 116 and 35 not out.

Bedi was eventually relieved of the captaincy after a disastrous series in Pakistan in late 1978 and at last Gavaskar was named captain for the series against the new look West Indian team (minus the pros engaged in Kerry Packer's WSC circus).

Between then and 1985 he led India intermittently in no fewer than 47 Test matches, but his overall match record can hardly be termed an outstanding one: played 47, won 9, lost 8 with as many as 30 Tests left indecisively drawn.

What, briefly, is the verdict of history concerning his tenure of the Indian captaincy? In assessing this, it is important to bear certain facts in mind and to consider the views of professional critics as well as his team mates and opponents.

That he was undeniably an accomplished and great batsman there can be no doubt whatever; his superlative statistics, his amazing consistency over the years 1971-87 attest to this, and though he was a student of the game and a knowledgeable player, he does not find a place among the great band of captains such as Douglas Jardine, Don Bradman, Frank Worrell, Richie Benaud and Mike Brearley.

We must keep constantly in mind that a number of highly accomplished batsmen, fit to be called great with a willow in their hands when the adrenalin was flowing and the mood was on them, did not make outstanding captains and never adapted to assuming additional responsibilities as leaders of men and tacticians in the demanding and challenging cauldron of Test cricket. Superb batsmen like Wally Hammond, Gary Sobers, David Gower, Bill Lawry and Ian Botham all have moderate records as Test match captains, for varying reasons.

An important clue to a fair assessment of Gavaskar as a captain lies in quoting what he himself has confessed about the onerous task of leading his country. Dom Moraes in his revealing book *Sunil Gavaskar: An Illustrated Biography* quotes Gavaskar as saying in an interview:

"Captaincy is something I never wanted. I didn't want the

responsibilities nor the hassles. I was proud to be captain of my country, but deep down I didn't really want the job."

A picture emerges clearly of the celebrated Indian opening batsman as a committed but reluctant captain. And in his "History of Indian Cricket" another Indian cricket writer, Mihir Bose, states inter alia:

"Though winning mattered to Gavaskar, he seemed not too enarmoured of his captaincy role, to the shrewd observer."

In support of the submission above that not all great batsmen necessarily make great captains, here is a list of the Test match record of seven modern captains:

CAPTAIN		PLAYED	WON	LOST	DRAW
Sunil Gavaskar	(Ind)	47	9	8	30
G.S. Sobers	(W.I.)	39	9	10	20
J.R. Reid	(N.Z.)	34	3	18	13
D.I. Gower	(Eng)	32	5	18	9
W.M. Lawry	(Aus)	25	9	8	8
W.R. Hammond	(Eng)	20	4	3	13
I.T. Botham	(Eng)	10	0	3	7

But are results in Test matches the sole criteria in assessing fairly the intrinsic worth of a cricket captain as a tactician or a leader of men? It certainly is not. Other factors need to be considered carefully.

But by the same token there are limitations to what a captain can achieve in the way of results, no matter how knowledgeable he may be and how shrewd a tactician. In the modern pace-oriented age of international cricket, it is undeniably a distinct advantage to have a fast bowling string to your bow, as England once had with Truman and Statham, or before the war, Larwood and Voce, or as Australia had with Gregory and Mc Donald, Lindwall and Miller, Lillee and Thomson.

For all the kudos handed out to Clive Lloyd during his memorable reign as the West Indies captain between 1975-85, how successful would he have been if he did not have on call a seemingly

At the Sheriff's office in Bombay, Sunil Gavaskar welcomes citizens of the state.

The masters together. Don Bradman and Sunil Gavaskar.

Is Boycott advising on perfecting the craft?

Sri Satya Sai Baba and Sunil.

In a lighter moment the Indian Cricket Team entertains.

Lord Relator, famous for his calypso on Gavaskar, presents an album to his hero.

Marshneil, Sunil and Clifford Narinesingh.

never-ending assembly line of excellent bowlers to throw at the enemy? .... Andy Roberts, Michael Holding, Joel Garner, Colin Croft, Wayne Daniel, Malcolm Marshall and Winston Davis, used at various times as an unrelenting four-pronged attack.

Gavaskar never had such ammunition to fight India's cause in Test matches. He was denied the scylla of speed to assail his opponents and had to rely on the charybdis of spin to eke out whatever Test victories came his way between 1979 and 1985.

With the best will in life, it was (traditionally for most Indian captains) an unequal battle and inevitably a war of attrition rather than an irresistible frontal assault against his opponents from England, Australia, Pakistan and the West Indies, especially when played on foreign soil.

It might be argued, of course, that the quality of India's spin bowling during his years at the helm was excellent, even superlative, and this is true. No other country was so rich in capable spinners. A roster of the main bowlers who did Test duty for India when Gavaskar was entrusted with the captaincy includes the names of revered spinners like Bishen Bedi, Dilip Doshi, Ravi Shastri, Maninder Singh (all orthodox left-arm spinners); off-spinner Venkatraghavan and the freak wrist spinner Bhagwant Chandrasekhar, all names to conjure with in the world of cricket. And most of the others (Ghavri, Binny, Chetan Sharma) were medium-paced. But there was little fast bowling support for these men until Kapil Dev emerged to revive visions of pre-war days when Amar Singh and Nissar (pioneer pacemen) starred for India.

The truth is, however talented the spin attack any team has, cricket history (traced back for more than a century) will confirm that usually it is the fast bowlers who win Test matches; and as a rule, they hunt in pairs: Larwood and Voce, Lindwall and Miller, Hall and Griffith, Peter Pollock and Procter, Holding and Marshall, Lillee and Thomson, Tyson and

Statham, Younis and Akram.

This is not to say that spin has not on occasion, been the decisive factor in the outcome of some Test series ....the names of Grimmett and O'Reilly (1934), Ramadin and Valentine (1950), Laker and Lock (1956), and Prasanna and Bedi (1971) are exceptions that prove the rule. But, more often than not, it is great pace that reaps the plums of victory.

Faced with this dilemma, then, it is not surprising that Gavaskar (like so many other Indian skippers) found it expedient to resort to defensive tactics in Test matches. Some critics would say "ultra defensive". He did not possess the "ammunition" to retaliate in kind or counter-attack effectively, and resorted to shrewd use of his spinners in his quests for victory, whenever it was possible. He did not have a balanced attack.

Vickram Singh in his book "Test Cricket: End of the Road?" states that Gavaskar's match record was one of the best among Indian captains but "his captaincy, like his batting at times, was rather defensive," but with good reason. He lacked the tools, the fuel to fight and this must exert a psychological effect on any captain.

This seemingly negative approach, though - whatever extenuating circumstances are quoted in defending it - is perhaps nowhere better illustrated than in the Calcutta Test of 1985 against England. In a match marred by rain, Gavaskar strangely delayed his declaration until India were 437 for 7 in the first innings, with much play already lost. This ruled out any chance of a result, and the Indian captain was the recipient of much heated criticism among his supporters. Gavaskar was actually smuggled from the grounds after close of play to escape the fury of the incensed crowd and it was alleged that he swore never to play at the Eden Gardens grounds again.

Yet, for all this, The Bombay cricketer took his captaincy very seriously indeed. The Yorkshireman, Don Mosey, a respected cricket writer, has laboured this point in his entertaining book

"The Wisden Book of Captains on Tour". Mosey writes:
"Gavaskar came close to creating an international incident which would have had disastrous consequences for himself and for Indian cricket. In the Melbourne Test of 1981 he was given out LBW to Lillee for 70 in the second innings, and disagreed so violently with the decision that he induced his partner Chetan Chauhan to quit the field with him............Fortunately, the Indian team's manager S.K. Durrani met the pair at the pavilion gate and ordered Chauhan to resume his innings."

Ironically, India won that Test (by 59 runs); but if Gavaskar had got his way, his team would have forfeited the match and his own blossoming career might have been permanently truncated as a disciplinary measure. This anecdote reveals vividly that Gavaskar was clearly a sensitive man of strong convictions. And then Mosey adds:
"Off the field, I found him a charming man, a shrewd business man, and an affectionate family man. He had strength of character- but on the field he was not too happy if things were not going his way.............. Tourists in India felt that Gavaskar, through his brilliance as a player, and his personality, achieved a certain dominance over Indian umpires. But he was a cosmopolitan and highly knowledgeable member of cricket aristocracy."
On that controversial Melbourne incident, Dom Moraes states that Gavaskar was "provoked into acting as he did by the bowler Lillee who allegedly made some abusive remarks" to the batsman after he appealed. Yet Moraes concedes that the Indian skipper, in encouraging Chauhan to come off the field acted in a reprehensible manner.

But what of the band of revolutionary thinkers who feel that such action by Gavaskar is justifiable as a counter to the abrasive and unsportsmanlike behaviour of Lillee?

Throughout his career Gavaskar was seldom far from the limelight of controversy and adulation. Raj Singh Dungarpur, who followed his career during the stages of its development is quick to speak of his outstanding captaincy and feels that he might have shared more of his immense knowledge of the game with the youngsters during his captaincy. But the constraints of the 'musical chairs' of captaincy may not have allowed that. The celebrated English commentator and writer, the late John Arlott, thought his captaincy record in his early years at the helm, an admirable one on the whole, but, he too, considered him, understandably defensive and cautious in his tactical approach. But Arlott adds: "And the inexplicable vagaries of India's selectors did not help." In praise of him Arlott continues: "He remains a seminal figure in Indian cricket history, a batsman with equable temperament, sound defence and unwavering concentration at the crease who never seemed in trouble against fast bowling."

Brian Johnston, another respected English commentator, stated that, in method, Gavaskar was a mixture of Bradman and Boycott, with an insatiable appetite for runs and with a near-perfect technique. "During his captaincy reign, he preferred in later years to bat lower in the order, leaving the initial flak to younger players. At home, he was the idol of cricket fans, adulated in Bombay like a film star."

Even a cursory glance at Gavaskar's career reinforces the belief that he stood firmly and resolutely in his decisions and was never a meek apostle to officialdom and the selectors. When his playing days were over, his journalistic career revealed that he was determined to express his views on the game fearlessly, even if it meant offending those who crossed his path. His syndicated column bears ample testimony to his outspoken criticism.

A glance at his writing indicate his scathing criticism of Lloyd's intimidatory tactics in 1976 and the Jamaican crowd's behaviour. On the controversial Pakistani umpire Shakoor Rana, in 1988, he stated that he was not "surprised that the whole of Pakistan is proud of Shakoor. He will rank along with Hanif, Zaheer, Imran and others for his undoubted 'contributions' to Pakistan cricket." It is a scathing comment with which Mike Gatting might agree. His reference to the Indian selectors as court jesters, his assertion that strangers should be banned from players' dressing rooms and his refusal to accept MCC membership are all indicative of a strong-willed character who was capable of defying the 'rules' of the game and abandoning the Melbourne match.

Distinguished players from various Commonwealth countries have spoken or written in glowing terms of Gavaskar's towering prowess as an opening batsman. That other living legend, Don Bradman, scion of an earlier era, called him "an ornament to cricket" and another, Australian skipper, Bobby Simpson, rated him as a very good batsman with limitless powers of concentration.

Former West Indian captain, Jeff Stollmeyer, who witnessed his remarkable debut series in 1971, stated in his autobiography, published in 1983: "Young Gavaskar put a stamp on each of the four Tests in which he played, imperturbable as a rock."

His batting has been lavishly praised by Pakistani's Zaheer Abbas and Mushtaq Mohammed, as well as his own teammates Wadekar and Pataudi. And needless to say, his wife Pammi, has been   supportive throughout his career.

But usually there were muted reservations about his status as a captain, even after making due allowance for India's paucity of pace bowling and often fragile batting. Perhaps it is the high percentage of drawn matches - 30 out of 47 or 63 percent.

Mike Brearley, shrewdest of English tacticians, praises his splendid 221 at the Oval in 1979 which almost earned India an improbable victory but rates his delayed declaration at Calcutta in 1985 as a bad miscalculation. His over-caution, Brearley feels, let England off the hook and he also blames Gavaskar for time wasting tactics on other occasions.

The Indian journalist, Ravi Chaturvedi, regards Gavaskar as a folk hero, a legend in his lifetime whose personality is, in a sense, multi-dimensional: batsman, author, broadcaster, columnist and articulate public speaker, as well as business executive, brilliant mimic with a wry sense of humour and an excellent team man on tours. He terms him a keen student of the game and "a man for all seasons".

But Bishen Bedi might not agree with the last encomium for he nurtured an ongoing feud with Gavaskar, fuelled no doubt, by the traditional rivalry between the cities of Bombay and Delhi and Bedi's belief that Gavaskar was responsible for his demise as a captain.

It was Gavaskar who had succeeded Bedi in 1978 for the home series versus the West Indies and he had shown that the onus of captaincy did not affect his batting form, scoring 732 runs (average 91) and clinching the series 1-0. He also won home rubbers against Australia and Pakistan in the winter of 1980, but thereafter he enjoyed only moderate successes until Kapil Dev came along. A wretched series against Pakistan in 1982-83 (lost by a 3-0 margin) caused the selectors to be disenchanted with his leadership.

But before finally relinquishing the reins, he led India to a thrilling but totally unexpected victory in the 1985 Benson and Hedges limited overs tournament, held in Australia. Placing the emphasis on fielding and physical fitness, he made his team a happy bunch who waltzed into the finals against Pakistan after reeling off victories against Australia, New Zealand and England. Cynics called it a fluke.

He surprised the critics by using the wrist spinner Sivaramakrishnan in an attacking role (previously an alien concept in one day tournaments) and his inspired gambit paid off. With fine performances from Shastri, Amarnath and Kapil Dev, India swept all opponents aside and triumphed over Pakistan in the final. Gavaskar demoted himself in the order and played some vital innings to set up the final euphoric challenge. After this he relinquished the captaincy to Kapil Dev, but starred as a batsman in another one-day series in Sharjah.

Vasant Naik has called Gavaskar "The Napoleon of cricket", quite justifying the sobriquet by claiming that the Little Master conquered everything he aimed at and did it convincingly. Both of similar height and both rose to dizzying heights in their respective fields. But Naik states that, unlike Napoleon, however, the Indian maestro never met his Waterloo.

This rings true to some extent, yet one feels that the changes in tenure of captaincy between him and Kapil Dev, and his unconcealed distrust of officialdom and the administrators of Indian cricket prevented him from cementing his hold on the reigns of captaincy. His tenure at the job was intermittent and this might have further influenced his reluctance in the role he was called upon to play, a role he did not seem enthused over.

Had it been otherwise, he would have appeared as leader in several more series, by virtue of his charisma, skill and ability to motivate his players. This I believe must be the verdict on Gavaskar. The continual constraints imposed on him certainly affected his performance as captain.

In the final analysis, Gavaskar may not have been an outstanding or successful captain, but it would have been interesting to watch him directing operations with a bowler like Imran or Lillee or Marshall at one end, and Kapil Dev at the other, with spinners like Bedi and Prasanna also on call.

The image of Gavaskar which endures in the memory is that of a well-organized batsman, dedicated to excellence and safety of method, and at his best, exciting in his strokeplay. Most cricketers would settle for such a resumé, and would regard any prowess as a tactician and captain a welcome bonus.

A total of 10,122 Test runs at an average of 51.12 is a laudable legacy for any batsman.

CHAPTER 10

Beyond The Playing Field

When a man goes out into his work
he is alive like a tree in spring,
he is living, not merely working.

When the Hindus weave thin wool into long, long
lengths of stuff
With their thin dark hands and their wide dark eyes
and their souls still absorbed
they are like slender trees putting forth leaves, a long
white web of living leaf,
the tissue they weave,
and they clothe themselves in white as a tree clothes
itself in its own foliage.

D.H.Lawrence.........WORK

The purpose of this chapter is to present to the reader the activities of Gavaskar the cricketer beyond the playing field. His absorption and quality of engagement in the game have elevated cricket to a meaningful realm and invested it with nobility. His loyalty and love for all that is cricket and the intrinsic value these experiences offer, add to a quality of life, enriching and sustaining. The critics will continue to harp on the financial rewards of his efforts but anyone who truly knows Sunil will attest to his passionate interest in all that surrounds cricket and will view him as a person whose loyalty to the game transcends the limits of materialism.

Gavaskar has not only distinguished himself as a batsman, but has gained wide acclaim for his prolific writing on his experiences as a cricketer. His display of physical dexterity with the use of the bat is complemented by his skilful manipulation of language as a tool of expression. He has been described as "busy outside the playing field as he is when at the crease." But his time is not confined to writing only, but to cricket commentary, business commitments, and social ceremonies.

This is even more evident now that he is in retirement. All his endeavours or efforts are expressive of a versatility, talent and keen sense of discipline.

For Sunil the sport was not an end in itself. It was not sheer physical dexterity, but it was fused with unflagging assiduity or mental absorption at the crease and beyond. The consciousness which developed was revealed in his desire to record, shape and communicate his experiences. So during his career he mixed desire with memory to recapture those experiences which impinged on his consciousness.

The first major attempt at recording his experiences is autobiographical in nature. Indeed all of his four published books are biographical in content for they all are about his cricketing life at different stages of development. In 1976 he blossomed into print with "Sunny Days". The book traces the direction of Sunil's development and his early achievements in the cricketing arena. In it, the author attempts to give order and structure to his thoughts, feelings and experiences within a realistic framework. The work is largely a record of his growing up, his entry into cricket, his education and his intermittent disappointments and successes as a young batsman, which have brought him to his current eminence as one of the world's greatest batsmen.

Sunil's illustrious career as a cricketer in general and a batsman in particular began with a 'bang' on his mother's nose which became the first victim of the novitiate's attacking strike, a strike which was later refined and redefined as the pride of the Little Master and the joy of the cricketing world.

Impelled by a creative talent and an analytic mind with a penchant for technical details, Sunil has brought to this work a wealth of knowledge and experience not only in the sphere of batting but also in other realms in the field of cricket. His objective evaluation of incidents and character, the variety and vividness of his descriptions, the fair measure of precision in his use of language and his fidelity to his subject all contribute to the distinctive quality of the work.

Through the author's vision is presented a gallery of human characters, each of whom makes his dramatic entry and exit in the theatre of the turf, performs invariably at all levels of excellence and stems the tide of public criticism, adulation or ridicule.

In its entirety "Sunny Days" reflects the author's growing consciousness of the strength and weakness of human nature and his sense of justice and fair play. The courage and sincerity with which he articulates his deep convictions, his humility in admitting failure and the modesty with which he enjoys success and fame are all clearly evident in this work.

In "Idols", his second work, the young writer pays tribute to some of the greatest cricketers in the international field. A close reading of the portraiture reveals Gavaskar's keen sense of observation, his penetrative insight and his extraordinary interest in cricket and in those outstanding cricketers whose performances have created history. His analysis of form, technique and style in bowling, batting, fielding and wicket-keeping of the various cricketers whom he admired, and his assessment of their social life off the field, have imbued the work with a wholeness, a balance which reflects the personality of the writer himself.

As one reads his various works, one discerns that precision which informs his descriptions, the graphic and vivid details with which he describes style and technique of players, and the fluency of thought and language. One is impelled to read on with the same avidity which one displays when looking at his batting performance.

In his delineation of the various characters he recalls memorable experiences on and off the cricket field, which were shared with men whom he admired and respected. He pays tribute to 31 of his fellow cricketers but he regrets the fact that the constraints of book size did not allow the inclusion of other cricketers whom he has admired during the years of his playing career.

In Alan Knott, Gavaskar perceives the finest wicket-keeper he has ever seen. He recalls with delight, Knott's brilliant wicket-keeping in the year 1971 when the Indian team toured England and played a match against Kent at Canterbury. Gavaskar recalls Knott's superb diving and his agility which make him unparalleled behind the wicket. He has great admiration for Knott as a person; his perpetual smile, his eagerness to communicate and his willingness to give hints and advice on technique or physical fitness deeply impressed the young Gavaskar and reflect his own values as a person.

The natural charm, diplomacy and versatility of Asif Iqbal did not fail to capture the attention of the observant writer. In "Idols", he expresses great respect and admiration for Asif's administrative ability and his desirable rapport with his teammates.

Greg Chappell's confidence, superb batting and his dignity of bearing in controversial issues make him a brilliant model to budding cricketers. Gavaskar considers Greg "the lynchpin around whom the Australian side was built."

Gavaskar considers Ian Botham to be England's greatest all rounder. His ability to stir the crowd, his efficient and smooth captaincy and the modesty with which he enjoyed fame and success are the distinctive features which the author respects and espouses.

Richard Hadlee's superb performance in bowling and his charisma are worthy of emulation. He is considered one of the finest new ball bowlers who has engaged in a Test match. His warmth and friendliness on the field make him an unforgettable person.

The author is also proud to have associated with two famous

cricketers, Rajinder Goel and Padmaker Shivalkar who were both left-arm spinners of the highest quality. Though they were never fortunate to have been selected to play in Test matches, their contributions to cricket must never be underestimated. Gavaskar admires them both for their skill, simplicity and modesty.

Gavaskar considers Sir Gary Sobers a cricketer with the greatest versatility. His excellent performance as a batsman, a bowler and a fielder has earned him this rare distinction. He has won the highest respect from the writer on whom he has made an indelible impression. Sir Gary's enjoyment of life and of cricket and the enjoyment he gave to cricket lovers are memories which the author will always cherish.

Rohan Kanhai, another stalwart in cricket is defined as "one's hero, one's idol' one for whom there is so much admiration." In the writer's judgement, Kanhai surpasses all others in his ability as a batsman. He is fond of Kanhai, not only as a cricketer but also as a person whose warmth, generosity and willingness to give advice he has often experienced. So great was Gavaskar's admiration for him that he chose to name his son Rohan and expressed the hope that someday he may follow in the footsteps of the great master.

The author has looked on with increasing interest at Kapil Dev's rise to greatness. His greatest success was achieved when he led India to victory in the Prudential World Cup. He is admired for his confidence, his modesty and his ability to lead the team by example.

John Snow is remembered for his skill as a fast bowler. His short, smooth and rhythmic run up distinguishes him from other fast bowlers. He has that aggressive streak when bowling to opening batsmen in particular. One famous incident which the author vividly remembers is when a ball from Snow struck Engineer's pad and went down to square leg. Gavaskar, while making his way down the pitch for the quick single, collided with Snow. He was sent sprawling and his bat was knocked from his hand. Fortunately, he managed to reach the crease with his wicket intact. Snow was made to apologize for this incident and was later disciplined.

Notwithstanding this incident, the writer finds Snow a good friend off the field. This is especially evident in their social encounters where they enjoyed friendly banter.

This work on the whole, reflects the author's prodigious power of organizing experiences and the exceptional wisdom, sympathy and understanding which emerged in the full tide of his cricketing career. His ability to mingle criticism with praise and to strike that fine balance between analysis and evocation is an achievement which undoubtedly belongs to maturity.

"Runs 'n Ruins", Gavaskar's third work constitutes a series of episodes in which are recorded experiences of India's encounters with Pakistan and the West Indies in India. The encounters followed in the wake of India's historic victory in the World Cup of 1983. The book is a revelation of the changing fortunes of Indian cricket which suffered a lean period following the splendid World Cup achievement.

The series between India and Pakistan ended in a draw and this was a morale booster to Pakistan who saw themselves equal in strength to the world champions. In the first Test at Bangalore, Gavaskar scored a century which served to boost his self confidence.

In this work Gavaskar again shows his capacity for evaluation, analysis and introspection. He attributes India's decline to several factors which directly and indirectly affected their performance. The monsoon rains in September interrupted play frequently and ruined the grounds. Preparation for Test cricket was inadequate since the euphoria of the World Cup victory had not completely worn off. An absence of team discussion to assess strengths and weaknesses of the team and those of the opposing team was also a contributing factor to India's decline.

India's first encounter with the formidable West Indian team came right after the drawn series with Pakistan. The one-day international match at Srinagar was an unforgettable experience for India. The crowd demonstrated their hostility against the Indian cricketers. It was for India a demoralizing and stunning experience.

Some of the greatest moments in Gavaskar's career were achieved against the West Indies and this he records in his work. His early dismissal at Kanpur in the first Test gave him the impetus to do all in his power to combat the fiery pace of the West Indies. He adopted a new style of batting. In the second Test at Delhi his adventurous style countered the demonic West Indian attack and in the process he achieved his 29th century, another milestone in his career. The final Test at Madras saw Gavaskar at the zenith of his performance. He achieved his 30th Test century and was given the Man of the Match award.

Though India suffered annihilation at the hands of the West Indies, Gavaskar stood prominent in his magnificent achievements and established a world record of thirty Test centuries. Despite his personal triumphs, he felt a sense of despair for it was "heartbreaking to find Indian's cricket magnificent edifice of June 1983 lying in ruins."

In this work Gavaskar attests to the greatness of the West Indian cricket team. There is, too, a personal feeling of optimism for the future of Indian cricket.

Gavaskar wrote his fourth book "One-Day Wonders" in 1985. It is essentially a graphic account of the Benson & Hedges World Series Cup tournament played 'Down Under' during the 1984-85 Australian summer.

The series proved to be one of the highlights of his long and distinguished career, in which Gavaskar's reputation as a captain was enhanced immeasurably. In a sense, this tournament was something like a farewell gift to limited-overs cricket.

It is a slender volume-the text itself is no more than 137 pages long- but it is eminently readable and interesting and devoid of any pretentious style: succinct, outspoken, witty, packed with anecdotes (both on and off the field), and full of human interest and behind-the-scenes intrigue.

The Benson & Hedges Cup was eventually won by India that year, a totally unexpected outcome as Australia had been favoured to win by the aficionados of the game, while both Pakistan and England had been more highly fancied than Gavaskar's Indian team.

The fact that India emerged victors came as a major surprise to the critics (both amateur and professional) as well as the Australian cricket public. One of the best chapters in "One Day Wonders" is the account of the gripping final against Pakistan in which Gavaskar out-generalled his counterpart, Javed Miandad.

The buildup to the tournament makes compelling reading, as the author reveals how he first heard of his appointment as captain, not from an official of the Indian Board of Control, but from his wife, Pammi! And the suspense leading up to this as he earlier waited in Ravi Shastri's hotel room for the announcement is skillfully created in chapter one of this book.

During the tournament, Gavaskar abandoned his familiar role as an opener, and batted in the middle of the order, as was his wont in the twilight years of his career.

Though the author is modest about his leadership qualities, it is obvious that his performance in Australia that summer gave an inner strength to the Indian team who reeled off victory after victory and won their group comfortably to qualify for the final. India's image in one-day cricket had received a boost - and to his credit, the author pays glowing tribute to several of his teammates: Srikkanth, Mohinder Amarnath, Kapil Dev and Shastri.

He also praises the indispensable contributions made by the cheerful wicketkeeper Satanand Vishwanath and all-rounder Roger Binny. On arrival in Australia for the B & H series, Gavaskar had laid a strong emphasis on fielding practice and physical fitness - and he is convinced his policy paid rich dividends during the tournament.

Another salient feature of the series was the shrewd manner in which leg-spinner Laxman Sivaramakrishnan was used by his skipper -in an attacking role, a rare ploy for a bowler of this type in one-day cricket.

India beat Pakistan, England and Australia comfortably and Gavaskar calls his triumph over his arch-rivals Pakistan "the icing on the cake."

The author stresses that the team's morale was high - and at the press conference after the final victory, Gavaskar chided the disbelieving critics in sarcastic and humorous vein!

Naturally, India were accorded a tumultuous home-coming - and then it was off to the Rothmans Cup in Sharjah where India's men won again, with Gavaskar named as Man of the Series. Two one-day triumphs in the space of a few weeks - and Gavaskar stresses in the book how proud that made him feel.

The reader's interest is sustained throughout this book, not merely in the narrative of the B & H matches - but also the clash of personalities, the controversy, the crowd's and Gavaskar's outspoken comments on administrators and press.

About the latter, the author states:
"My disappointment lies in the fact that the media often make up stories which have no basis in truth."

The book deals with some of the controversies which plagued his career - clashes with the Indian Board of Control and his 'rivalry' with Kapil Dev, often blown up and grossly exaggerated by a news-hungry, sometimes malicious press. As Gavaskar remarks, it is a pity the public tend to lap up everything written about cricket, accepting it as gospel truth, not frivolous fancy.

After his active playing days were over, Gavaskar embraced cricket writing as a new passion - and this love of the game and the urge to write about it is reflected in "One Day Wonders", a book which reveals the author's knowledge of cricket tactics and lays bare his own idiosyncrasies and enthusiasms.

As Gavaskar grew in stature as a cricketer and made an impact on the game, Indians looked to him as a role-model, as one to be emulated with pride. Everyone was thrilled and fascinated and genuinely expressed admiration. The business world recognized his value, worth and ability. This led to endorsements, advertising contracts, presentation of T.V. serials on cricket with Gavaskar as host and narrator, cricket commentary, writing of sports columns and the demanding agenda of social functions.

As early as 1973 advertising cameramen observed the special quality of his presentation and he was seen as an advertising symbol. He has made advertisements for products such as shaving cream, shades, hair dyes, polish, clothes and sportswear; even his son Rohan has made appearances with him.

Gavaskar became India's advertising sensation with his successful advertising projects. The advertising agents talk of his universal appeal and charisma. To them he seems to adjust admirably to the variety of products he advertises. Dinesh Suitings have featured him over the years. In the advertising world he is not only a cricketer but a national celebrity.

The agencies and companies which are associated with him are given total freedom to extract all the shots and images they need. They are happy for there are no obstacles, no additional demands from him, and are satisfied with his conditions and remarkable business transactions. Indrani Banerji and Rajana Kapur in their research into his activities beyond the cricket field report on critics who see "Gavaskar's entrepreneurship as an instance of commercialism which is unbecoming of a cricket star." But Ajit Wadekar, his cricket colleague and former captain, counters this criticism and justifies the use of Gavaskar's celebrity status.

What is most revealing about his appearances in advertisements is his appeal to the audience. Indrani Banerji and R. Kapur claim that "his presence has an appeal and yet for some undefined reason, does not overpower the product message." One of the advertising cameramen explains: "He does not have to be directed, and, on his own, manages to focus on the product he is endorsing." It is very evident all the success that Gavaskar achieves can be attributed to his sharp mental aptitude and intelligence coupled with a commitment to the task at hand; an absorption that is manifest in all his efforts and pursuits in life.

In the field of business, he is part of the popular Sunny Sports Boutique. This company is partnered with the responsible Raju Mehta and the former Indian Women's cricket captain, Shubaji Kulkarni. The outlet distributes Sunny's sporting equipment and full range of sportswear, including his designs, to a wide market.

One of the more challenging and enterprising activities is Gavaskar's involvement with PMG, Promotional Management Group, an organization which focuses on protecting the business interests of stars. It is a company partnered with Sumed Shah and it also enlists the services of director Marshneil Gavaskar. This enterprise started with the objective of assisting cricketers in their contractual arrangements with advertising firms. Now other celebrities are managed by the group. In Gavaskar's words: "It is an all-star management group. We will manage their endorsements and take care of all the legal aspects." The company does not make contractual arrangements with individual stars but advises advertising agencies and clients on appropriate sportswear for their campaign. It takes care of these details and is remunerated for its role.

On its agenda, is the promotion of other meaningful and entertaining activities. For instance there are television serials such as the musical serial on ghazal with an array of notable singers, the selling of sportswriting columns written by famous cricketers including Imran Khan, Allan Border, Viv Richards, Jaisimha, Ravi Shastri and Sunil Gavaskar to newspapers. The television serial *Gavaskar Remembers* features Gavaskar at play, interviews held and his memories of past games. The other well-received serial of 13 programmes, entitled *Sunil Gavaskar Presents* illustrates a committed person with natural ability not only for the game but with a mental and intellectual involvement. This absorption and dedication are qualities suited for good presentation and in this respect he has demonstrated an ability to narrate with fluency and ease. This experience was of great delight to the directors of the programme who gleefully recalled "the words just seem to flow like his delicate strokes."

It is remarked in Bombay that Gavaskar's celebrity status has not changed his simple, modest life-style; he remains a self-effacing, compassionate person. His wife Marshneil has grown accustomed over the years to his simple eating habits, his abstinence from alcoholic drinks and cigarettes. He reserves the right to an occasional champagne. This discipline, however, does not restrict the use of alcoholic drinks when he entertains friends and family at his spacious, homely and comfortable apartment at Worli Sea Face.

During Sunil's active cricketing years he promised to make himself available and to assist in the interest of fellow cricketers or retired ones. In retirement he ensures that he is free and accessible to the needs of cricket benefits. It is encouraging to read Banerji's and Kapur's special report of his commitment to benefit games during his active career:
"Once after landing in Sahar from Sharjah, Gavaskar went on directly to the domestic airport, took a flight to Hyderabad, got off and climbed into a bus where he slept through the overnight journey, finally reaching Vijayawada in the morning, ready to play a benefit match for retired Ranji Trophy player Mumtaz Hussain. Similarly, he rarely misses the Bombay Kanga League matches when he is in Town."

It is interesting to note that Salim Durani, a remarkable cricketer, who served India's cricket in the late 50's to early 70's looked forward to a benefit match to subsidize his earnings. The

Illustrated Weekly of India May 23/24 1991 reported Durani's statement:

"What I am looking forward to is my benefit match in April. I am entirely depending on my friends and colleagues like Sunil Gavaskar and others to assist me in this."

Durani's mention of Gavaskar is significant for it indicates the respect cricketers hold for him; he was and is always there to assist and show appreciation for his colleagues and he has had a special respect for Durani, whose generous spirit and magnanimity he fully recognized. Gavaskar's willingness to acknowledge his colleagues makes him endearing to them.

Among his friends there were diverse opinions on his celebrity status during his retirement. There are those who see the need for him to develop an independent image free from cricket. Suggestions are rich regarding a permanent television anchor role in sports. But he seems satisfied with his stints at commentary during cricket and his journalistic essays on the game. And one wonders whether he really needs to retain an image, to make a deliberate effort to recapture centre stage position. In reality he does not.

Sunil has always handled success and celebrity status with dignity. One commentator describes his attitude towards it as "earthy". He was always pleased with his celebrity status but also recognized that the nature of that glamour was not permanent and he had no problems with that. Before retirement he responded to an interviewer "I feel quite nice to be a celebrity and to be recognized in the streets or anywhere else but I know that in a few years there will be someone else who will be enjoying the same position, the same attention."

In anticipation of his retirement he appreciated his success and felt it "important to be able to bask in its warmth when your days are gone." Retirement to him he felt "may be it will be the most blissful time of my life," for he often yearned, "to retreat to a corner and live the life of an ordinary man. And believe me, it's an overpowering feeling."

The yearning for privacy and tranquility, to create his own 'Innisfree' in Bombay, to revolve around his intimate family circle and friends is understandable when one considers the tremendous sacrifices in meeting the demanding duties of Test cricket. He often missed spending "a Divali at home or New Years with my family and friends." He was also away on tour in New Zealand when his son was born.

There are many prominent figures in India who strongly advocate a role for him in the politics of India. In this he has no interest though he shares some refreshing ideas and thoughts for his country's development. Some see him as a representative of his country in the diplomatic services, perhaps assuming ambassadorial duties. And then there are those who think that knighthood is a most deserving award for his significant presence in the cricketing world. He did usher in a new renaissance in Indian cricket. The spectrum is wide and varied. But though retired from active cricket his desire is for a coaching school in cricket. This is where he needs support so that he can explore and optimize the possibilities of such an undertaking. Whatever his role in retirement, be it sport or social work, his intense involvement is remarkable and inspiring.

Now that Sunil is away from the very bright lights, there are still demands on his time but he is able to cope quite comfortably with societal demands. But he may be happier if he is perceived or recognized as Sunil the person, the friend, not only as Gavaskar the star, the television personality or public figure.

CHAPTER 11

The Faltering Hero?

.... that these men, -
Carrying, I say, the stamp of one defect,
Being nature's livery or fortune's star,-
Their virtues else, - be they as pure as grace,
As infinite as man may undergo, -
Shall in the general censure take corruption
From that particular fault.

William Shakespeare: Hamlet

Shakespeare's tragic heroes are presented as characters whose thoughts, deeds and actions have elevated them to grandeur and great eminence. They are admired for their heroism, bravery, courage and nobility of mind. But in the process of life they suffer in a tragic manner, their end or destruction caused by a particular flaw in their character, a flaw for which they are not wholly responsible; it is, as Hamlet reflects, 'a vicious mole of nature' which in spite of great virtues, reduces them to abject misery and a tragic end.

The allusion here is not to portray Gavaskar as a tragic hero; indeed, there is no tragic condition. It invites us to view him as a person who has emerged heroic in stature, excelled in his craft as a batsman and who through his thoughts and actions beyond the cricket field, evinced nobility and humanity. It calls on us to consider him as a figure not immune to the glow and blast of the passions, one whose 'controversial presence' did at times arouse critical indignation.

The picture which stood out was that of a man at the centre of controversy, with strong opinions and ideas. At times he was misunderstood and misrepresented.

His critical attitude and occasional scathing remarks incurred

162

the wrath of officials, cricket administrators, umpires and the press. It was felt that his stance was too authoritarian and revolutionary, and his declarations or pronouncements were attributed to youthful impetuosity and arrogance. But he always stood firm, he always showed tenacity, resilience and courage in campaigning for cricketers' interests.

The aura of his individual personal presence and prolific achievement earned not only respect but aroused awe among his peers and contemporaries. With the spectators, a love-hate relationship developed; he was communicating or interacting with a people whose expectations knew no limit and who never seemed to have allowed him a 'humanness'; it was a people who loved his prowess infinitely and fanatically; they felt he could not err. When he did, their admiration or devotion was transformed into indignation and bitterness. This negative feeling was most apparent in their behaviour.

While we recognise his all-round contribution as a sportsman and individual and elevate him to the grandeur of heroic status, it will be unjust and unfair if we do not view him as one who has been the subject of adverse criticism from some critics of the game, contemporaries and most notably some sections of the media. These view him as the faltering hero, fallen from grace and esteem through irrational statements and actions and selfish motives.

It is compelling that an attempt be made to view these 'misdemeanours and shortcomings' with objectivity before we consign him to the flames or make him the servant of Sisyphus. It is in this context that significant incidents and issues which sparked off controversies and criticism are addressed. It is hoped that through this exploration greater insight into his character will be derived.

One of the fiercest piece of criticism levelled against him grew out of his conduct on the field when playing against the Australians at Melbourne. On this occasion, Gavaskar as opener and captain, was batting splendidly when an LBW decision was ruled against him, much to his disappointment. This 'unfair' decision coupled with the profanities of Lillee, the Australian pace bowler, almost precipitated an end to the match when Gavaskar called on his teammate, Chetan Chauhan, to walk off the field. It was through the intercession of the manager that Chauhan was sent back and play resumed. India eventually won this match.

Gavaskar writing in his book "Idols" a book which celebrates the feats and achievements of cricketing greats he admired - Lillee included- gives a full explanation of the incident in order to clarify the issue.

In his account Gavaskar implies that his reactions on the field then, could have been attributed to a series of events which contributed towards building up a state of tension which perhaps rendered him vulnerable. The team as a whole had been disappointed with the umpiring of Whitehead whose decisions many times were unfavourable to India, and had requested Gavaskar to do something about it. One of the players, Kirmani, had hinted to him that if Allan Border was not given out the previous day when he was bowled by Shivlal Yadav, he would have walked off the field. Gavaskar then told Kirmani that he must abide by whatever decisions are made and by this he implied that he would not condone walking off the field. Psychologically the words "walk out" had registered in Gavaskar's mind.

Prior to the incident, Gavaskar admits that he had just started to enjoy that feeling of confidence and optimism in the wicket when he played a ball from Lillee with the inside edge of his bat and the ball went on to strike the pad. This he said, triggered off an appeal from Lillee for leg before, and finally Gavaskar was given out. At this point Gavaskar was seething with anger and as he was walking off the field Lillee's profane utterances caught his attention. He then told Chauhan to walk off the field with him. Lillee's profanities he felt precipitated this erratic and unfortunate reaction.

EST INDIES, AVED BY UNCOVERED' VICKET..!

Disappointed Sunil Gavaskar, I feel cheated ..!

LIE MURPHY
W DELHI,
nday,
UTER-CANA]
INDIA'S policy
not covering Test
tch wickets cost
m the fifth Test
ainst the West
dies, here, toda,
hen only two an
half hours play
were possible on a
right sunny day.
wicket, ring

"My current hero is Kapil Dev"

Sunil Gavaskar tells TOOSHAR PANDIT

hat is it like to be a
keter in India? Is it satis-

Well, I think it is nice
a cricketer in Indi-
ar the most po-
ry. Cricke

Their hearts
than wi
O.

The West Indi
394 rel

FACE TO FACE

EXCLUSIVE INTERVIEW: SUNIL GAVASKAR

'Why I Got Mad at Melbourne'

sort of person. An
few instances he f
handle was at Melb
when he walked off,
conceding the Test. A

MID-DAY

OPINION

Understandin
Gavaskar

A CRUCIAL cricket match involvi
dia, in which a fit and in-form Ga
does not figure, has about it an air
reality that is disorienting in the ext
Millions of cricket-lovers from t
try's troubled Northern Frontier to i
tioning Southern shores will want te
cile their sympathy for his own feeli
their disappointment over his optir
the Indian side.
The instant and natural reactio
be to fault him for his decision.
mould in which fate has cast Sunil
— not only as a cricketer h
vidual — is so sn
to d

NIL GAVASKAR

THE MISUNDERSTOOD MASTER

e it a
their
non-will
m

ACCESSIBLE.
Down to ear
intelligent.
Somewhere alo
the line, he is al
one of the more
human superstars.
Is possibly one of th
few things for which
he has never been
credited. It is
something one
begins to appreciate
when one turns to
'he glamour bo
abro

almiya lashes out
Gavaskar's stand

Staff Reporter
ta, Feb. 8: "The Calcutta
does not need a c
f good h

availability for the W
final at

Sunil Gavaskar talks exclusively to The Telegraph

I need a bit of privacy'

of playing for his country un-
less the re
were pretty
good?
Greg Ch
Mike B

with TV beaming
body's living roo
see for oneself,
need certificates
of this official's
What I need

'I am a human being,

nave even been booed in my
re in Bombay. So

I was dumbfounded
when told about
omission —Gavaska

From Our Special Correspondent

GWALIOR, Sept
"I was dumbfounded" said Sunil Gavaskar
when asked how he reacted after being told by
his father that he was dropped for the Jaipur ar
Srinagar one-day internationals. The greatest
accumulator of runs and centuries in Test crick
Gavaskar had gone to his father's house at Dada
on Sunday to wish him on his birthday and giv
him a gift, after playing in the Kanga league
match. Instead of being blessed, what Gavaska
received from his father, Manohar

Selectors' volte-face
Gavaskar reinstated

Kapil Dev was omitted from a one-day international
ame Test against England, the selectors (four of
ee served then too: Man Mohan

Gavaskar considers this incident most regrettable and his behaviour, unsportsmanlike. He accepts responsibility for his action and admits that no provocation should have evoked such a reaction. He should have controlled his emotions on the field and given vent to it in a more appropriate place like the dressing room.

Gavaskar recalls that after the Test, some Indian and Australian players were invited to a dinner, among whom was Dennis Lillee. At that dinner Kapil asked Dennis why he was so abusive on the cricket field and Dennis replied:

"It's because I am a fast bowler and when I bowl a bad ball or see the batsman edge without result, my frustrations come out in the open. Because there is so much more effort to be put into fast bowling than you medium pacers are required to."

Gavaskar believes that it was this attitude on the part of Lillee that made him such a renowned fast bowler.

In a climate that is suggestive of hostility there are always instances where players find it difficult to transcend their emotions and so they fall prey to temptation, to visible and aggressive expressions of anger and outrage. However, in moments of sober introspection, they do sound the note of regret for their human limitations and realize that private individual feelings must be subordinated in the interest of good sportsmanship.

Another major disappointing incident to which Holding makes detailed reference, in his book "Whispering Death" occurred in Madras in the final Test in the series between India and the West Indies in 1983 in which was witnessed a momentous landmark for Gavaskar. In this Test Gavaskar surpassed Don Bradman's record number of centuries, having reached his thirtieth with a score of 236 not out. According to Holding, Gavaskar, prior to this eventful occasion, had been experiencing a few disappointing innings and was subjected to criticism from the media and many of his supporters. At Calcutta his response to the first ball of the match cost him his wicket and in the second innings he actually gave up his wicket with a devastating shot. These failures resulted in his request to be put in at no. 4 in the last Test. Holding thought that this move was indicative of Gavaskar's loss of confidence and that Gavaskar had not really gained by a change in the batting order since the first two wickets fell without a run; India was placed in an unfortunate position with 92 for 5 in response to West Indies 313, when Gavaskar apparently edged a ball from Marshall, sending it to third slip. The ball kept low and Harper took a 'catch', but Gavaskar stood firm and the umpire ruled in his favour. Holding believed it was a glaring mistake on the part of the umpire and in retaliation they boldly showed their disapproval by not recognizing Gavaskar's various achievements during the innings. The press was critical of the unsportsmanlike behaviour of the West Indian team, but it failed to mention anything adverse about Gavaskar's sportsmanship in obtaining a not-out decision, when to Holding it was a 'clear catch'.

Holding admits his annoyance at contrary decisions of the umpire and confesses that the feeling is aggravated when the batsman is of the calibre of Gavaskar. In his experience, Gavaskar is the most difficult batsman to dismiss especially if the conditions make him comfortable in the wicket. Holding says of Gavaskar:
"He was very sound and technically correct, and like the other great opposition opener of my time, Geoff Boycott, had tremendous powers of concentration."
By not recognizing the historic achievement of Gavaskar, the West Indies team suggested that they had cast negative judgement on his character and had openly condemned him. But was this reaction or concerted effort to express displeasure fair to Gavaskar? How certain were the West Indians of the 'dismissal'? At that particular time he was not bothered by, nor did he seem aware of their reaction but subsequently in his publication of 'Runs 'n Ruins' he gives a faithful account of the incident:

"Marshall was to bowl the first over of the morning and his second ball was short and came at my face like a rocket. Instinctively my hand shot out to protect and put the ball down. The ball hit my forearm protector just above the wrist and flew in the air and as Harper took the ball, the West Indians jumped up thinking they had taken my wicket. The umpire, Swarup Kishen, confidently rejected the appeal and I breathed a sigh of relief. The appeal was confident and the sound of the ball making contact with the forearm protector is the same as when it hits the gloves and so I was worried as I looked at Swarup Kishen. I still have the mark of the ball on the forearm protector to prove this, because so far that has been the only time I have been struck there."

His home crowd recognized him as a stalwart on the field and he always tried to live up to their expectations. He had always been known to walk if he felt certain he was out; his heroism allowed for no dishonest ploy. Moreover the benefit of the doubt always goes to the batsman and in this particular case Gavaskar was not given out. He himself has admitted that there is only one team against whom he will not walk without the umpire's decision and that is Pakistan, for he has suffered incessantly at their hands.

During the West Indies tour to India in 1983, Gavaskar recorded his 29th Test century to equal Bradman's record. He was now on the threshold of a great historic event. To eclipse Bradman's record would be a feat worthy of his stature and it was felt that his 30th century was just a matter of time. In the Test at Calcutta, a crowd of approximately 90,000 looked on as he was dismissed for 0 off the first ball he faced. In the second innings he began with great aggression and confidence only to fall to a reckless stroke for which he paid dearly. The century was denied him and the crowd's anger was intense; not only was its rage and venom directed at him but his wife, Marshneil was subjected to open hostility. Missiles and oranges were hurled at her. This public humiliation and embarrassment together with his personal failure and the suggestion that his recklessness at the wicket was a deliberate attempt to undermine Kapil's captaincy, could only infuriate and throw him into distemper. His response to this criticism will be explored later in this chapter.

In the 1984-85 Test series against David Gower's team, Gavaskar experienced the humiliation of the crowd's anger at Calcutta when he delayed the declaration of the Indian's innings thereby allowing the match to peter out into a tame draw. The apparent consensus of opinion was that he should have declared earlier and given England a challenge; a sporting declaration which would have lured them to take up the issue, thus creating the scene for an exciting and tense conclusion.

Sports critics firmly believed that India could have afforded to risk this match; it was already trailing 2-1 and it was up to India to act decisively. In defence of his strategy he thought there was no chance of defeating England had he declared earlier. He saw no merit in thrusting them into such a challenge for it would have yielded no decision. However, the crowd's tolerance waned when faced with a meaninglessly prolonged innings with no prospect of excitement or decision. The result was a constant roar of disapproval and chants with Gavaskar as the target of their frustration.

It was reported that Gavaskar, in response to the crowd's attitude and behaviour, made a very telling statement that he would never play a Test at Calcutta again.

Two years later his decision to opt out of a Test at Calcutta, the second Test against Pakistan, met with resentment and rage, both from the press and the public. The following is a newspaper report (The Calcutta Telegraph) on his decision:

> *'SUNNY OPTS OUT OF TEST IN CALCUTTA'*
> *Madras, Feb 6: Sunil Gavaskar will not play in the second Test against Pakistan beginning in Calcutta on February 11. He told newsmen here today that he had written to the Board of Control for Cricket in India (BCCI) saying that he was unavailable for*

the test as well as the one-day international to be played at the Eden Gardens on February 18. In his letter, Gavaskar cited "personal reasons" for his inability to play.

Asked what he would do if he was still selected, Gavaskar said he would not be present in Calcutta during the Test and if the Board selected him in spite of his categorical letter, he could do nothing about it.

Gavaskar, however said " I am available for the rest of the season. I will not be available for the matches at Calcutta. That is all."

Gavaskar's decision not to play in Calcutta is ostensibly a reaction to the crowd's behaviour there during the third Test against England in 1984-85, when the ace opening batsman, who was then the captain, was reportedly "booed, insulted and abused" for his late declaration of India's first innings. At the end of the Test, Gavaskar had categorically told newsmen that he would never play in the city again.
Gavaskar's announcement came shortly after he had scored 91 in an opening partnership of 200, which spurred India to 290 for two at close of the third day in the first Test against Pakistan here."

Reactions were widespread and condemnatory. An incensed public, discontented press members, some of whom had the pleasure of prior conflict with him, and administrators were loud in their rhetoric and openly outraged. Bishen Bedi in his report expressed that the personal reasons which Gavaskar cited for his non-availability was an indication of his personal discomfiture against the rowdy elements which follows cricket in Bengal. He went on to express disgust with Gavaskar's decision, for here Gavaskar was not thinking of the national interest. An enraged Jagmohan Dalmiya, the vice-president of the Cricket Association of Bengal (CAB) quipped "The Calcutta crowd does not need a certificate of good behaviour from Mr. Sunil Gavaskar." He went on to justify the crowd's behaviour; it was a direct criticism of Gavaskar's strategy that precipitated the incident.

The incident developed into a highly emotional and dramatic issue. The emotional and passionate spectator, the skeptic, the cynic, the well-intentioned critics all expressed their views strongly and at times passionately. The press and public perceived him as a hero who had alienated himself from his people; while they recognized and appreciated his distinguished and illustrious career, some viewed his decision as drastic, unkind, selfish, void of maturity, unbecoming of his stature; and others even appealed to him to reconsider and forgive the past incident.

An active media, in this instance, the Telegraph, conducted a survey seeking reactions from a cross-section of Calcuttans.

The following pieces are expressions of disappointments, representative reactions of the general climate of opinions:

> *Sujoy Chakraborty (DC, Central): Unfortunate though Gavaskar's decision is, I think it is not justified. The entire Eden Gardens crowd cannot really be blamed if a section of it showed its frustration. Nevertheless, I think half the charm of the Test will be lost because of Sunny's absence. This is a very depressing thought.*

> *Babi Nobis (race horse owner): In the nation's interest Gavaskar ought not to have decided to give Calcutta the skip. He has obviously taken the whole affair too personally. He could have been more mature. I won't be surprised if the wound is reopened the next time he plays in Calcutta at any level of the game. In the interest of his legion of fans here he ought to revoke his decision.*

> *Samar (Badru) Bannerjee (ex-Olympic footballer):*

In his book "Sunny Days" Gavaskar had mentioned his dislike for Jamaica's Sabina Park's crowd behaviour. He wrote about them in very strong terms, yet he did go back and play there. Had he done the same here he would have done his image no harm. If anything, he would have won the hearts of fans here. Unlike some people, I do not think ticket sales for the Test will be affected by Gavaskar's non-availability.

Sukumar Samajpati (ex-football international): Gavaskar would have come out as a greater sportsman had he forgotten the distasteful incidents of the last Test and come over and played here despite his 'vow' not to do so.

Subimal Dasgupta (Joint Commissioner, Armed Police): If the treatment Calcutta fans meted out to Gavaskar on the last two occasions is the reason for his giving the Test here next week the skip, I'm afraid he is being unkind to all of us. The behaviour of a small section of the thousands at the Eden Gardens should not be reason enough for his drastic stand. Efforts should be made by anyone who loves the game to persuade this great cricketer to reconsider his decision. His absence may have a bad impact on the image of this sports loving city. I wonder whether Gavaskar will boycott the final of the World Cup here in Calcutta if: (a) he retains his place in the team and (b) If India make it to the final. If Gavaskar really does not play in next week's Test here, I shall miss him.

A more balanced opinion (The Telegraph, February 8, 1987) was expressed in this editorial:

"Calcutta's spectators have not behaved well with Sunil; true. In the 1983 series against the West Indies they objected to the manner he got out against Marshall and showed their displeasure when Sunil's

wife Marshneil came onto the ground to speak to Doordarshan, at the end of the match. In the series against Gower's England team Sunil was booed again, as much for his play-safe captaincy as for the past memory. Well, if Calcutta has a long memory, so has Sunil Gavaskar. He has now acted upon the vow he took then never to play in Calcutta again. But is it right to take such a step to display displeasure against that section which protested? After all, Sunil Gavaskar has a duty to the team too: if his absence leads to defeat, will Sunil Gavaskar be forgiven? And finally a player who has got so much adulation and respect from everywhere should, surely, learn to take a bit of booing in his stride.

Come on, Sunil. We will miss you. Calcutta may be temperamental, but behind the temper it has a very warm heart. You have made your point with your statement; and we understand. Let us forget the past and return to the game. Come on, Sunil. Be a sport".

This 'opinion' is rational, sympathetic towards his plight but also questions the reasonableness of his action and his commitment to his team which he should consider. It makes a gentle appeal to him for a change of decision.

Amidst the controversy, Gavaskar broke his silence and gave a full statement clarifying his position on the matter. He claimed his reasons were personal and private and that the conclusions made that the crowd's antagonism was the reason for his unavailability is unfounded. He had been booed elsewhere in India; he further suggested that his absence may be due to "a medical check up or a religious ceremony. May be plain mental and physical fatigue and the desire to rest for a week. Why do people presume it is because of booing? Is it because of a guilty conscience?"

What he maintained was that his reasons were personal and private and he wished they would accept that. "What I need is for people to understand that I am a human being and if I need a bit of privacy I should be allowed that. If I need a bit of time to be left alone, then I should be given that."

In his concluding statement critics discerned a touch of diplomacy or even a conciliatory gesture:
"If my reasons are personal, let them be so. After all, if you look into it carefully and dispassionately the greatest loss is mine. If my fans in Calcutta are going to miss me then let me say in conclusion that I am going to miss them too."

Media personnel and the public viewed his public disclosure negatively; they felt it was an inflexible will at work countering all their enticements and appeals for him to play.

In the light of Gavaskar's seemingly plausible explanation citing personal constraints which affected his participation, could it be deemed with absolute certainty that he avoided the game because of his past experience at Calcutta? Could it be that his reasons were genuine and real? Or are we to make moral judgement on his action? Couldn't he be experiencing deep inner crisis of spirit? Is it possible with the unwelcome confrontation, he experienced tragic 'aloneness'?

Had Gavaskar succumbed to the public pressure and decided to play, then all arguments denouncing his inflexible will, condemning his lack of patriotism and national pride, granite pride and aloofness, image and reputation, would have ceased. The 'crowd' would have restored his image, for in their blinkered vision the immediate satisfaction of entertainment was their prime interest.

Instead Gavaskar did not yield to vigorous opposition and the pressure of circumstance. One commentator felt it was his pride and will to stand up for what he thought were his principles; not even the voice of reason or logic would change his mind. To this critic it was a perversity, a perversity that accompanies genius. Whatever his reasons, he stood forthright, maintained an apparent calm, fixed and constant in his decision.

The Midday newspaper in its Opinion page, perceived the

issue as one of greater complexity than playing for the delight and excitement of the crowd:

> *"A crucial cricket match involving India, in which a fit and in-form Gavaskar does not figure, has about it an air of unreality that is disorienting in the extreme.*
>
> *Millions of cricket lovers from the country's troubled Northern Frontier to its questioning Southern Shores will want to reconcile their sympathy for his own feelings with their disappointment over his opting out of the Indian side.*
>
> *The instant and natural reaction would be to fault him for his decision. But the mould in which fate has cast Sunil Gavaskar - not only as a cricketer but as an individual- is so special that they will hesitate to do so before pondering the problem.*
>
> *Artists are sensitive, the greater, the more so. They flourish in an atmosphere that is conducive to their art. Where this is not forthcoming, they could be cramped and stultified not merely to their own disadvantage but to that of the art and the cause, and of those who derive pleasure from it.*
>
> *The great Little Master's desire to keep out of the Calcutta Test must therefore be considered from the point of view of the eventual overall advantage it will bring, rather than the immediate gain that people expect from it.*
>
> *Nothing could be farther from Gavaskar's mind than to defy the Cricket Control Board or to let down his country. This is proved by his willingness to play in Calcutta should India be in the World Cup final later in the year.*
>
> *In a game that calls for both discipline and pride in one's country, Gavaskar could hardly have risen to his present position if he did not have these*

qualities in ample measure.

Those who disapprove of his action should balance it with what he has done for Indians over long years - the glory that he has brought, the joy that he has given - and try to understand the difficulty and agony of his choice.

Yet there is no getting away from the wistful thought, what a grand thing it might have been, what a wonderful thing, if he had achieved the record of completing 10,000 Test runs amidst the plaudits of that same crowd whose jeers he had feared.

Will it yet come to pass? Millions of Indians in India and abroad must hope that it will.

The Midday, in defending his sense of patriotism and his contribution to India's cricket tries to define the nature of the sporting experience in the larger context of art and artistic achievement. Gavaskar must be seen not only as a cricketer, but as an individual. The atmosphere, the setting, the total 'landscape', must be ideal and not counter-productive, must not stultify creativity. The predicament in which he was placed, the negative circumstances surrounding the issue would have affected his performance, his craft, his art. Perhaps his retreat from the madding crowd could have been the best form of action.

Whatever the arguments for or against his absence from the game, the fearful memories of degradation and humiliation, the oppressive nature of such an experience could have lingering effects on his mental frame. Such experiences can do moral and spiritual harm and make it difficult for sincere communion with the outside world.

In Ashok Kamath's words "controversy has always been to Sunil Gavaskar what the little lamb has been to Aesopian Mary: a diligent follower. And in the Little Master's case, with controversy and excellence has been attendant adjectival excess."

He has been adored in superlative and flamboyant language and criticized with the same intensity of feeling. Kamath continues:

"Part of the Gavaskar's legend's colour comes from his celebrated brushes with authority, the press and fellow cricketers."

Without reservation, moral judgement, negative and destructive found expression through the pens of the critics who labelled him materialistic and mercenary. But it was also Gavaskar's candour, aggressive and forthright stance on significant issues which earned him negative responses. His comments on the press or sections of the press' habit of misrepresenting the facts, the fragmentary information from unreliable reports, negative and sinister, disturbed him. The battle he fought did not end on the playing field against the fiery pacebowler or the guile of the spinner, but with the armoured pens attacking unrelentingly.

To the public he was presented as mercenary, demanding lucrative rewards. In the light of this indictment, it must be said that Gavaskar possessed the independence of spirit, the courage, fortitude and determination so characteristic of him, to make claims and justify these claims for the progress of cricketers as professionals, claims which were not only monetary; and this he did with professional equilibrium.

In the Foreword to "A History of Indian Cricket" by Mihir Bose, Gavaskar says:

"Players have always had to play with a Damoclean Sword hanging over their heads. It could fall on them not only because of their cricketing form but for reasons unconnected with the happenings on the field. To perform in spite of this additional pressure is no easy task. In fact, it is often easier to guess what international bowlers are going to bowl than what the Board is going to throw at you! This lack of understanding, due to unwillingness to have regular dialogue with the players, has been Indian's cricket greatest tragedy. No test player has ever been at the helm of the Board, indeed the Indian Board must be the only Board of Control in the world which has non-cricketers, not just occupying the highest positions on the Board, but also representing various affiliated associations. A cricketer's viewpoint is thus seldom, if ever heard. He has no control over playing conditions or other matters important to his performance. I mention this only to emphasise how the deeds of Indian cricketers have to be seen in this light when Indian cricket history is being written."

It must be mentioned that he was not only critical of the Board's policies and practices but was also aware of its openness to young players. It has given the opportunity to improve and develop skills and in this it is comparable to any other part of the world. It is at the international level that problems arise.

With the conviction that sportsmen, especially the average players, were sacrificing the major part of their younger days concentrating on the game without significant rewards, he rallied to their cause; he saw to it that they derived additional benefits from the game.

It was Sunil's profound belief that excellence must be rewarded in order to motivate and unearth more excellence. Before his entry into cricket, Test players were subjected to the Board's terms and conditions. It is through his initiative, his will to secure greater benefits for the players, that the present group is enjoying satisfactory rewards - increase in payments for games, endorsements, advertising contracts, well-paid jobs in most cases at major institutions, firms, corporations and banks.

In an article published in the Week November 15-21, 1987, the writer clearly identifies Gavaskar's priorities in respect to the game:

"In all his writings and other statements, Gavaskar has been explicit about his thinking on three inter-related themes: first it is the players who have made the game so popular and rich in this country; secondly, a player's career is perforce short and risk-prone; thirdly, a former player is like yesterday's newspaper, discarded and ignored. He worked on these three themes systematically to ensure for himself and his fellow

cricketers a clout and a standing which many officials have still not reconciled themselves to."

In addition to the advantages gained by current players he encouraged young players, opened up employment opportunities for them, thus making it possible to earn a living and also pursue their cricketing careers. With this new initiative, firms and companies joined in the encouragement and support for players by offering satisfying jobs. His commitment to the game and continuing pursuit ensured that he found time for the youth. In the midst of busy schedules he made sure he spent time with the youth team before they embarked on a trip to Australia.

Another commitment he has not wavered from is his continuing support to former players through his presence and participation in benefit matches. However crowded his agenda, he accommodates these occasions, together with the countless occasions for charitable causes.

The fact that Sunil is so inextricably woven into the fabric of his society, its cricketing activities, societal commitments, moral commitments to different fraternities, would lead one to ponder and question whether the judgement of him as mercenary is really an uncompromising assessment of his character. It would be noble of us to address these issues with openness and genuine receptivity of mind.

Sunil's conflict with the press disturbed him. He recognized honest reporters and believed that players and reporters could together contribute to the progress of Indian cricket. In his early chapter in "One Day Wonders" he cites instances or incidents of glaring and most galling reports of misrepresentation but he prefaces this by saying:
"I have no complaints against the press for their criticism of my cricket and captaincy. That is the way they see it and even if I do not agree with them I will certainly not hold it against them. My disappointment lies in the fact that they make up certain stories which have no basis in truth."

He was genuinely perturbed by irresponsible reporting with its sole motive of defaming his character, image and reputation. He cited the incident with Kapil Dev after they had lost the Delhi Test and Kapil was omitted, pointing to the press' disregard for truth. The assertion of the press he emphatically denied: "The papers reported that after Kapil got out in the second innings there was an altercation when he returned to the dressing room. The truth is that not a word was said by either of us. While I was certainly disappointed and upset by his mode of dismissal I knew there was no point in saying anything, because it would not have made Kapil go back to bat. Yet the papers made a big issue of a non-event and had recourse to evasions like '*alleged altercation*' and '*according to dressing room sources*'.

By the way, the discussion to drop Kapil had started before I joined the selection meeting. I was late joining the selectors because I was urging the players to forget the Delhi disaster and look forward to the remainder of the series as a 3-Test series. My opinion was certainly sought when I did join the meeting later, and it was given in no uncertain terms, but again, it was I who got the sole blame for Kapil's omission."

Another incident relating to Mohammed Azharuddin's success sparked off bitterness between Sunil and the press. During the Kanpur Test when Azharuddin made his third consecutive century, the Hindu Paper posted a boxed news item stating that Sunil Gavaskar did not applaud Azharuddin's achievement. Sunil denied this and expressed hurt especially as this report was published in the *Hindu*, a top drawer, which would not normally malign somebody without checking the facts. In the following piece of his writing taken from his book "One Day Wonders" he gives a plain detailed account of the incident: "I was in the dressing room and watching the game on the T.V. there when Ajju turned the ball off his hips to take the single for his century. The moment I saw that he was going to complete the single I ran outside applauding the achievement. Obviously I could not be seen in the front because everyone was standing up and clapping and it's not my style to push and come to the front to get attention from TV cameras or photographers. Yet the press, sitting on the opposite end of the ground, made it an item of sidelights of the game that I did not applaud Azhar's feat. Nobody bothered to check with me but went ahead and wrote, because Gavaskar was everybody's favourite whipping boy by then."

His resolute denial of the charge and expression of the emotional effect such constant attacks had on him revealed a disheartened Sunil. He had become 'everybody's whipping boy'. Instead of being purveyors of truth he saw the press as being irresponsible traders of news, misleading and damaging in the process. But on a more positive note he called for a code of conduct to prevent the press from misreporting and misrepresentation. Though he was receptive to journalists (some of them would deny this) the impression created was that he harboured the thought that animosity towards him was well orchestrated. There were those, he felt, who deliberately dishonoured him in print by transforming trivial and non-issues into sensational reporting, magnifying minor events into major news items, issues and incidents more imagined than real. This to him was unhealthy and profoundly disturbed him. The image of the Colossus on the cricket field which signified his supreme batsmanship, the all-conquering hero of outstanding feats, was diminished into the unsubstantial. In the eyes of the media the Colossus was now aloof and imposing in the presence of his cricketing colleagues; he had distanced himself with a conceit and arrogance as if spurning the underlings. This was certainly a strong and harsh criticism of a man adored and respected by a vast majority, many of them to the point of hero-worship and fanatic obsessiveness and even fawning obsequiousness.

The media was focussing on what appeared as a feud between Gavaskar and Kapil Dev. It must be mentioned that Kapil Dev was one of the heroes of the game whom he admired. This he declares unselfishly in his evaluation of cricketing greats in his book "Idols".

The imagined feud was a fabrication of some media personnel suspicions of the nature of the relationship in which captaincy reversals between Kapil Dev and Gavaskar could have precipitated problems. Most of the reporting on the relationship between these two was mere conjecture. When Gavaskar was replaced as captain by Kapil Dev and then eventually re-instated the media felt there was hostility between them. Gavaskar accused the media of hiding behind its protective armament with its favourite shields *'allegedly, said to be, according to close sources'*, and openly requested the media to produce an authentic report on the 'imagined' feud.

Gavaskar recalls the genuine admiration he had for Kapil Dev, the friendship between the wives and denies any real confrontation or strong disagreement with Dev. They, as two individuals, unique in their cricketing talents, would have had differing views but this does not necessarily cause conflict. It could have led to a greater understanding of the more complex issues of the game.

During their playing days Gavaskar remembers:
"But in those days a lot of things were written. And again it did make a little sense to people who followed the game. Because when I was captain, when I was reappointed captain, Kapil's performance was not exactly top-drawer. And when I had been dropped as captain and he had been made captain, my performance wasn't anything to set the stands on fire. So I think there was the feeling that, okay maybe, we were not trying our best, which is ridiculous, because you know the one thing people seem to forget is that you have a personal reputation to maintain as a cricketer. If you've achieved something, that is there to maintain. Nobody in his right mind would deliberately play badly to let down a captain or a team. Because at the end of the day you're only cutting your own feet off. If you play badly you get dropped. Its as simple as that."

In response to his criticism of Kapil's performance in 1979 when he said that Kapil would not score another innings of 50 runs Gavaskar responded by saying that it was meant to be corrective. He had repeatedly admonished Kapil about his batting style and advised him how to make full use of his natural ability, for it was being wasted by careless impetuous play. He recalls:

"And I said I don't think Kapil will get another 50. And it was meant only to provoke him to get a 50 and come and tell me Skipper I got a 50. And he did that."

Kapil Dev was stung by Gavaskar's remarks. Though he later realized that Sunil had been critical in order to motivate him, he was hurt. He had preferred his captain had spoken to him privately.

On another occasion, Gavaskar expressed hurt and disappointment when Kapil Dev made comments about players whose interests were diverted to other matters away from cricket (at this time Sunil had failed at the crease but had kept his commitment on the 'rest' day to autograph one of his books in Calcutta). On the very same occasion during the Test match Gavaskar was full of praise for Kapil Dev's daring and courage amidst the violence that erupted at Calcutta.

It is interesting to note Kapil's view of Gavaskar during their cricketing relationship. Kapil had played over 40 Test matches under Sunil. He described his captaincy as a safe one. He never really took up a challenge. He believed in a simple principle: if we get an opportunity, we should try and win, otherwise play it safe.

There have been differing views on this subject which have already been explored in the chapter on captaincy. Kapil in writing of the Gavaskar-Dev relationship during his captaincy, felt that Sunil at the beginning was a little stiff, but he says "our relationship smoothened out, subsequently, despite all press reports. Quite frankly, towards the end, I often went to him for advice and he gave me all the benefits of his considerable experience." Dev continues "we developed a healthy relationship between ourselves."

In writing of another incident in their cricketing life Kapil recalls a highly charged and tense dressing room scene after he had done some short pitched bowling to the West Indian batsmen. In response to Chetan Chauhan's question: "Now who is going to face them when they start bowling short?" Kapil was stunned and could not reply. Sunil only returned a cold stare. Kapil realized what the mood was like and it was Sunil who broke the uneasy silence by reassuring words. He appeased Kapil by saying that his bouncers had not created any new problems and the wicket was such that the ball was always likely to come chest high or higher.

Any fair exploration of their relationship would reveal that there is no reason to label it as discordant or to condemn either cricketer. There has been a considerable amount of distortion and deliberate corruption of facts and this was done because the see-saw of captaincy afforded critics opportunity to draw their own conclusions. Gavaskar as a true cricketer has always affirmed that criticism of cricket and performance is positive once it can be justified and once it is divorced from attacks on personalities.

If the Gavaskar-Dev feud was more imagined than real how do we respond or react to the much publicized conflict between Gavaskar and Bishen Singh Bedi? Here was the existence of a healthy relationship during the earlier part of their careers with a mutual respect for each other. Bedi had revealed a strong loyalty by naming his son after Gavaskar. But much to the regret of many, their fellowship was marred by distemper and impulsiveness. The conflict intensified, more so, after their playing days.

Mudhar Patherya in an article entitled "Mister Controversy" discusses among other issues, Gavaskar's role as a captain and the measure of ill-will he accumulated from spiteful quarters (especially for his role in selecting players) and indicates that

Gavaskar may have opened himself to the critics but Patherya emphatically declares "If Bishen Bedi has any grievance, this is wholly misplaced. His allegation a couple of years ago that Gavaskar hatched a conspiracy against him has no foundation. If the then skipper removed him from the side, and he probably did, the former had every justification for doing so. The great left-arm spinner, after his display in Pakistan and against the West Indies in 1978-79 was rather lucky to make the trip to England the following summer. His arm once classically straight was no longer upright and that devastating incoming ball was virtually a thing of the past."

In spite of their disagreement Sunil always maintained a deep respect for Bedi as a top class bowler. In his " Idols" he recognizes him as the greatest left-arm bowler, and as one whose bowling caused plenty of havoc to batsmen all over the world.

During the latter part of his career he was the target of many criticisms from Bedi, which he prefers not to elaborate upon. Eventually matters worsened during the incident when players were banned by the Board. Bedi, in support of the Board's actions, charged Gavaskar for his control of the players and their counter plan. He said that the players were under the villainous guidance of the chief coordinator Sunil M Gavaskar. An angry Gavaskar felt that Bedi had overstepped his limit and therefore could not tolerate it any longer. The conflict escalated with Gavaskar questioning Bedi's integrity.

"I knew Bishen's duplicity, double standards because I had experienced it over a period of time. What he said and what he did were totally different things."

Gavaskar's emphatic defence was that the 'Hindu' had influenced the players decision.

"You know I had nothing to do with it (the players) their changing their minds, changing their stance from this to that. It was the 'Hindu' opinion had done it, but yet without making any enquiries, chose to accuse me."

It is significant to note that Dilip Vengsarkar confirmed that

Gavaskar had no part to play in the incident.

With the use of their syndicated columns to rectify matters and resolve differences, Bedi continued to attack and dismissed issues which Sunil had brought to his attention.

During the 1990 Test at Lord's, Bedi was manager of the Indian team; Azharuddin the captain, having won the toss decided to allow England to bat on what appeared to be a good batting strip. This decision was bewildering and perplexing to many critics of the game. Azhar faced the brunt of the criticism and Bedi, the manager disassociated himself from the captain's decision. It was rather strange for the manager to be ignorant of the captain's decision. Gavaskar, a commentator at that time, unleashed an attack on Bedi and this was followed by a verbal exchange. This fed the critics with ammunition to explode on both ex-players. It was felt that rivalry existed between them during their playing days and that Bedi had perceived Gavaskar as a challenge to his captaincy. In fact, after Bedi's crushing defeat in 1978 at the hands of Pakistan, he was relieved of the captaincy and Gavaskar was then appointed.

Vickram Singh, writing on Test cricket, "The End of the Road", lamented the fact that their conflict became the spectacle at Lord's. Gavaskar was critical of Bedi's management, his over-emphasis on physical conditioning, and his strange disassociation from Azhar's decision and his unbecoming remark on the Indian team. Some felt his attack was personal while he responded by saying it was a cricketing criticism, emphasizing the fact that Bedi should have done a bit more damage limitation instead of adding to the damage.

"My criticism about him as a manager was there. That he didn't do ....That he wasn't there to put any tactical input into the team, he was only a trainer."

In his apartness from the decision taken by Azhar, it was felt, according to Harsha Bhogle's reporting of the incident, that Bedi had deserted the ship at a time when it needed his presence most. He copped an amazing amount of criticism.

But the person whom he directed his venom against was Sunil. An issue to which Bedi took offence was Sunil's refusal to accept M.C.C membership. This many felt was not an issue for Bedi to pry into. It was Gavaskar's decision and it was personal; he had refused acceptance of membership because prior to this he was offended by an M.C.C official.

Gavaskar's decision was construed by outsiders as arrogant, strong-willed and emotional. Bedi's infuriation manifested itself in a letter expressing his disgust at Gavaskar's refusal of membership. The letter was distributed to the British Press and contained scathing lines such as "I personally feel quite disgusted and ashamed I ever played cricket with you."

This breakdown in their relationship was clearly a sad event in their lives. Here were two great cricketers, men of international standing, men in whom one could discern a solidity of character and an endearing, genial spirit, pitted against each other.

Any analysis of incidents or events which reveal insights into character, must be done with objectivity, integrity and a delicate sense of reasoning. We must hold the mirror up to nature, show virtue her own feature, scorn her own image. Any departure from this approach would inevitably lead to harmful, vulgar and insincere judgement.

Sunil Gavaskar, a cricketing hero with a career wondrous and attractive as it may appear, was never free from controversy. His intellectual courage and sincere articulation of his conviction did occasion a fair measure of negative responses and rhetorical condemnation from stern critics who unrelentingly undertook continual investigation and probing into all facets of his life. The private man and the public figure found no divorce.

Sunil has made his claim upon posterity and cricket is indebted to him. His achievements have been extraordinary and imperishable. As a private person there is no indication of pomposity; his bearing is of a polished simplicity, compassionate and supportive in human situations. Though at times he has been viewed as impulsive and impetuous, the media has never made life easy for him in their continuous and sustained war.

Perhaps in our assessment of Gavaskar's life and career we should not "make the background of gold against which to set up the real portrait, the picture of his increasing nobleness," nor should we take "pleasure in smashing the whole instrument on which the music of humanity has been played." Our critical analysis needs not the extremes of embellishments nor crude indignation. What is needed is balanced judgement and sincere critical commentary. It is only then that an appraisal will be responsible and free of insularity and prejudices. Only then will we aspire to the condition of truth.

CHAPTER 12

Present Times

Some work of noble note, may yet be done.
Lord Alfred Tennyson: Ulysses

S unil Gavaskar's achievements during his cricketing era as a batsman in the classic mould have elevated him to stardom; he has been canonized and immortalized in a Bradmanesque fashion and made imperishable through the literature of the last two decades. His unique technique and artistry were features of his batting which would inspire the muse to consume him into an artifice of eternity.

Cricketing history is replete with illuminating analyses of aspects of his technique and craftsmanship. Grandiose and at times outlandish allusions, analogies, conceits, hyperbolic descriptions fill the pages of cricket books, magazines, periodicals all attesting to his achievements in elevating batting to the aesthetic realm.

The periods of his cricketing days in which he experienced failure met with criticism, especially from sceptics in India who raged a continual war with him. There were descriptions of failure and gloomy displays; even portrayals of a flawed hero emerged, some with balanced judgement, others with sharp-knived threats. But Gavaskar, the supreme artist always emerged heroic in his conquest. He was able to show his critics that he could counter the most lethal pace attack and guileful spin bowling with ease and comfort.

Now that he has bequeathed a rich legacy to the world of cricket, his retirement confines him not to a lotus-like existence. It is filled with an unending stream of commitments.......... business, matters pertaining to the state coupled with his personal and family life. In his preface to 'Sunny Days', his early autobiographical account of his cricketing experience and development, he reflects:

"I have been singularly fortunate in so far as I have received the love and affection of cricketers and cricket lovers in abundant measure. On the cricket field and off it, I have made so many friends that I feel truly 'rich'. When I think of this, I am reminded of the famous lines of the poet Rabindranath Tagore:

> "Thou hast made me known to friends whom I knew not,
> Thou hast given me seats in homes not my own
> Thou hast brought the distant near
> And made a brother of a stranger."

Many years have passed and now in retirement it is appropriate to relate his experience to that of Ulysses (the Greek hero, immortilized in Lord Tennyson's poetry). Ulysses, in the twilight of his career, waxes lyrically about his exploits. His speech (monologue) truly reminds us of Sunil's adventures.

> "...........................all times I have enjoyed
> Greatly, have suffered greatly, both with those
> That loved me, and alone; on shore, and when
> Thro' scudding drift the rainy Hyades
> Vext the dim sea. I am become a name;
> For always roaming with a hungry heart
> Much have I seen and known: cities of men
> And manners, climates, councils, governments
> Myself not least, but honoured of them all".

Though now Sunil says he prefers aloneness and a private, tranquil life free of complexities where he can read, listen to music in relaxation and comfort and find time for his badminton, his activities indicate that for him:

"It is dull to pause, to make an end
To rust unburnished".

It is in this context that it can be affirmed that he has begun his "second innings". There is that indefinable, undying urge to give of himself meaningfully for he is a man deeply conscious of the forces that impinge on him; his is a vision that encompasses and comprehends the realities of life in his country and the development of cricket for the future. And he has expressed the wish to occupy his time with social work; there is in him that great measure of seriousness, reasonableness, practical intelligence and consciousness needed to address issues and problems which confront him. One can envision his future role in society, an active role in the alleviation of distress and the quest for more meaningful existence among his people. An indication of this is his interest in the handicapped and his visit to their schools.

At present, his appointment to the post of Sheriff of Bombay commits him to the role as a representative of the state. It is a position free of political affiliation, but his duties span the range from the ceremonial and formal to civic responsibilities of his state.

In addition Gavaskar is summoned to all parts of India on cricketing activities such as benefit matches, T.V. commentary, fund-raising ceremonies and social occasions. It is pertinent here for us to get an insight into the nature of his time spent in retirement. The following piece is part of an interview with Bertram Contractor held at the Nirlon House, where Gavaskar worked as a Public Relations Officer up to the mid-eighties. This interview which appeared in *Afternoon on Sunday,* January 1, 1995 gives a simple account of his activities:

Gavaskar: I write my columns here, meet people, do whatever personal work I have to do. Mondays to Fridays I am here, writing in longhand, the office then transcribes and sends it. When I am on tour, outside Bombay and abroad, I still write in longhand and fax it. Then I ring up to check if they have any problems with the copy. It is expensive, calling from abroad. But they are coming out with a desktop that recognizes handwriting and turns it into printed copy. I shall go in for that, it will make life easier...The rest of the day, yes. I have lunch at home, then go to the Bombay Gym for my badminton, 45 minutes to an hour. Then to PMG (Professional Management

Group) for whatever work there may be, TV projects, event management, sponsorships. The evenings, it depends, either at home or to some dinner I may be invited to. I do travel a lot, though for two to three months now, there are no travel plans. There are so many of these matches of seniors, then there are television assignments. I am travelling more now than when I was playing. And, since most of the time it is one-day matches, you are travelling every alternate day. When you are playing Tests, you stay put in a town for seven days. But I am fortunate, whether it is 'Sunny Sports Boutique' or anything else, I have got very good colleagues who work extremely hard. That gives me the luxury of hardly working."

Of great significance was his role in May 1995 in Trinidad, West Indies when he was instrumental as the co-ordinator, in organizing an Indian team made up mainly of Test players on a tour to Trinidad to play three invitational one-day matches against a West Indian 'A' team. This particular tour was part of a cultural celebration taking place in Trinidad. It marked the 150th anniversary of the arrival of Indians here. Together with Hemant Waingankar, the manager of the team, he was able to assemble the cricketers (notwithstanding the inherent problems ....mainly geographical and prior commitments) for a one week tour and this at short notice for a task of this nature. For him the visit did recall nostalgic feelings and it was thrilling and exciting as he walked around the grounds of Queen's Park Oval reflecting on his successful encounters with the West Indian battery of cricketers.

It was a return to what he calls his second home, the locus amoenus; a lovely place where his historic career began, and to a people who have shown since 1971 an amazing depth of appreciation and adulation for his heroic efforts and his endearing personality.

The reception accorded Sunil in Trinidad would have fascinated anyone present; indeed it amazed the young Indian cricketers who saw how well-loved and considered he is in Trinidad. And at all times he lent dignity to his presence on the island, meeting friends, renewing old acquaintances, signing autographs for old and young alike, responding to television and newspapers' reporters willingly and readily with calmness and composure. One of the highlights of the tour was the tribute to him in song, the calypso sung by Lord Relator. It was Relator's burning ambition to sing in Sunil's presence that memorable calypso of 1971 in which he lauds the Indian victory over the West Indies and in particular the young Gavaskar's success.

For not one moment was Sunil unruffled by the almost ceaseless requests for autographs. On one occasion the sprightly Avinder (Chico) Bharat in her characteristic innocence and pride in her country of birth (India) and her hero, requested Sunil's autograph on a miniature Indian national flag. Though appreciative of her enthusiasm, his sense of patriotism and commitment to his country would not allow him to desecrate the sacred symbol of the flag. But later, when he realized that one of the cricketers unwittingly gave away an Indian cricket cap he was disturbed and almost alighted from the bus on which he was travelling to recover the cap. He stated very firmly that he would give someone another cap or memento but not the cricket team's cap. To him it was sacrilege to treat your country's prized possessions with such indifference. He later reflected:

"You don't give away something of that nature, something you have earned, something that is part of you and your country." It was a lesson he had learnt from his cricketing uncle very early in his childhood.

Like Milton's poetry, Sunil's career is a doctrinal to a nation and both their lives and careers are a sustained triumph of will. In an article entitled 'India's Victim Mentality ...... The Importance of being Gavaskar', Gautam Adhikari calls on Indians to relinquish the victim mentality, one of the worst dangers of colonialism. Adhikari discerns a self-confidence and self-discipline "which have slid into a state of entropy over the centuries". This assessment echoes Jawaharlal Nehru's "The Discovery of India" in which he laments:

"Life became constrained in a prison of its own making." Adhikari cites Gavaskar as a symbol of a new thinking, an easy self-confidence and an astounding self-discipline, all of which are clearly demonstrated in his performance and accomplishments over the past 20 years.

Through his development as a cricketer and a person, Gavaskar has revealed to his country the quality of his heroism, his ability to confront, summon courage and resist with assurance and strength. From the batting crease, on the playing field and beyond the field he has made a statement which reassures Indians of their strength, endurance and dignity.

Essays on Gavaskar

PETER ROEBUCK

Greatness is never merely geographic. A bowler taking wickets only on the patch he's occupied since his cradle days isn't worth a rupee. A batsman comfortable only on pitches familiar since youth isn't worth a dime. True batsmen can score runs on damp, green surfaces that grumble beneath thick blankets of English cloud; they can score runs on rock-like pitches in Perth, on turners in Colombo, on hot afternoons in Calcutta and freezing mornings in Dunedin; they score runs against pace and spin and seam and swing. Nothing defeats them, or not for long anyhow.

Sunil Gavaskar was a wonderful batsman, one of the greatest to adorn an extraordinary game that encourages individualism yet wraps itself in the clothes of collective endeavour. As a boy, almost, he hit umpteen hundreds in the Caribbean, as a veteran, almost, he punished fierce Australians on their own carefully prepared pitches, a feat beyond most contemporaries from any part of the world let alone a man whose cricket grew on the Indian sub-continent. Such were his powers that he'd have been productive 50 years earlier or 50 years later; even in this hurrying world some things do not change, the principles of batsmanship not least amongst them.

Gavaskar was possessed of an unusual and potent mixture of wilfulness and technique, a combination that allowed him to endure the terrifying expectations of a vast, seething and sometimes fanatical nation. Occasionally his wilfulness could get him into hot water, for this was a mind capable of straying beyond the parameters of ordinary conduct, parameters he neither respected nor advocated, and into the realms of ruthlessness open only to those whose drive takes them beyond considerations of tomorrow's headlines and into battles of higher and lower matters, battles at once grand and petty. So it was that Gavaskar was to be seen leading his partner from the field one day in Melbourne after an especially harsh leg before decision had befallen an already unfortunate team. So it was that, during the 1975 World Cup, Gavaskar was to be seen defending as if for his life at a time when India were supposed to be chasing an improbable target. Typically, too, this misadventure occurred at Lord's, a place whose patrician leanings periodically brought forth infuriated conduct from a man prone to fits of democracy. Typically, too, Gavaskar was unrepentant, and redeemed himself on his final appearance at that distinguished ground, on a happier occasion, with a hundred so brilliant that those fortunate enough to witness it will never forget it. Here is a robust personable, sometimes contrary often masterful genius.

Gavaskar's first trip to England occurred in the early years of his glory, in 1971, at a time when Indian batsmen were not highly regarded overseas, "They can score runs at home" was the general opinion "But they aren't much use when it's cold and damp." Gavaskar arrived as a young man proud of himself, and of his nation, a young man determined to prove that he and his countrymen were made of sterner stuff. At the heart of his performances throughout his career could be found this desire to show that Indians could no longer be brushed aside; he wanted to tell the world that the days of charming, wristy and delicate cricketers were gone, and never to return. He set out to bring steel to the silky webs of Indian cricket. It was an endeavour in which he succeeded magnificently. Before Gavaskar, Indian teams were expected to lose and their batsmen were expected to crumble. Since Gavaskar, opponents know that Indians will put up a fight, at home or on foreign terrain.

Already, it is true, he had scored heavily against the West Indies, but that was not quite so difficult, then, as it is now. To arrive in a wet English spring and to find such astringent bowlers as Hendrick, Willis, Old and Underwood at the height of their powers, was to face a test utterly unfamiliar. No wonder Gavaskar in the contemplation of retirement, speaks proudly of the century he scored at Old Trafford in those bewildering first months of 1974. He's even called it the best innings of his career, a tribute, perhaps, owing as much to its significance as to its particular merits. After all, he had known he could score runs against England's most dangerous bowlers on a surface helping them. A task beyond most batsmen familiar with such circumstances, let alone a lad from Bombay who'd hardly seen such pitches before and could scarcely know what to do upon them.

If he could score 100 on this green and growling surface in Manchester, what might not be within his capability? It is a point well taken. England bowlers were to see a lot more of him, and in conditions more sympathetic to batting.

Helped by a miserable May, England won that series 3-0 but Gavaskar had proved himself to be a batsman of skill and concentration. He instilled combativeness and confidence in his team mates, rather as Clive LLoyd did in the West Indies, and he insisted that nothing was to be given away. Perhaps it made his captaincy a little conservative, for he lacked the killing bowlers, but India needed this fierceness of mind if it was to survive in the ever hardening world of cricket.

In 1979, India toured England again, and in a kinder summer it lost the series 1-0. Had luck not betrayed the visitors on the last afternoon of the final Test match, played at The Oval, India might have left with honours even. Chasing 440 or so, India reached 221 before losing a wicket, Gavaskar and Chauhan punishing the bowling to all parts of The Oval. Gavaskar himself scored 221 before losing his wicket to his old friend and rival Ian Botham. It was an innings much praised by old stagers who compared its mixture of judgement and technical prowess to the greatest innings played by Len Hutton. To see Gavaskar bat, in that match, was to see a player whose feet took him into perfect positions, whose head was unfailingly still, a batsman playing every ball at the last possible moment.

It was a masterly display and a shaken England were lucky to escape with a draw.

Not, of course, that this close Test series was the only cricketing drama of 1979. West Indies won the World Cup again that year, and Viv Richards scored 100 in the final. They were unbeatable. India, of course, didn't do much, weren't much good at one-day cricket, lacked the powerful batsmen, athletic fieldsmen and tight bowlers necessary for success within its brief confines. They'd never be any good at it - would they? Four years later the Cup was held in England once again, and India arrived with some experienced batsmen and a bunch of crafty medium pacers, most of whom had played in England, either during the mostly undistinguished visit in 1982 or by regular trips to the Northern Leagues. No one thought much about them, and India scarcely survived its match with Zimbabwe, Kapil Dev leading a remarkable fight back that took them from the perils of 25-5 to an astonishing victory. No one thought much about India even as they beat England on an amiable pitch in Manchester to reach the final. Few thought they had the slightest chance when they were bowled out for 183 on a surface smiling upon seamers. "They've had it," was the general opinion. Even in India, surely, the flame of hope flickered low. Incredibly, though, the West Indies fell apart and great and long were the celebrations at home. Gavaskar did not have a particularly productive World Cup, and it was not until his later years that he scored his first 100 in limited over internationals. A brilliant century made against New Zealand in his swan song year of 1987, at last taking him to a landmark he had long craved.

It was nearly over for Gavaskar. One more famous match remained, the celebration staged on a placid pitch at Lords between the greatest players in the world. Much to his disappointment, Gavaskar failed to score in the second innings and had not umpire Dickie Bird been in a generous mood, he might have scored a duck in the first innings too. Spared, Gavaskar proceeded to bat in breathtaking style, playing a stream of superbly executed strokes and so confirming his enduring stature.

And so it ended as well as it had begun. Apart from his visits with India, Gavaskar also played a season of county cricket with Somerset during which he contributed two of the finest innings I've ever seen, a century against Sylvester Clarke at The Oval and a scintillating limited over 100 against a powerful Middlesex attack that almost took his team to an apparently impossible target. Somerset learnt to appreciate his batting and his company. Sunil adapted easily to the genial ways of this tranquil part of England, and seemed to enjoy living and playing without the pressures that attended his every word and his every innings throughout his magnificent career in India.

Gavaskar left something of himself in Somerset, a gentler part necessarily subdued otherwise in the interests of scoring runs and satisfying the awesome demands on himself and his people. He left something of himself in England , too, and enhanced the respect in which Indian cricket is held across the land to which the game owes its origin. No longer can Indian players or Indian teams be taken for granted.

MIKE COWARD

Any Gavaskar retrospective elicits a range of emotional responses from the Australian cricket afficionado.

There is, of course, an overwhelming sense of pleasure at having seen the Little Master in full cry the length and breadth of the island continent the poets call the wide brown land. After all, 920 of the 1550 runs he scored against Australia (at an average of 51.66) were gathered Down Under and he is a member of that happy band to have scored a Test hundred at each of the mainland venues - Brisbane, Perth and Melbourne when the cricket world was at war in 1977-78 and at Adelaide and Sydney eight summers later when the focus of malcontent within the game had shifted from Packer to Pretoria.

For good measure he scored three more hundreds against Australia in India - two in his beloved city of Bombay and another at Delhi - and a daringly imaginative 90 which provided the impetus for the fantastic fourth innings of the tied Test match at Madras in September 1986.

Indeed, only against the West Indies, the power brokers of the modern game, did he score more hundreds. The fact that 21 of his 34 centuries were achieved against the West Indies and Australia surely is eloquent testimony to his greatness. There is, at the same time, a profound sense of regret if not resentment at being deprived of opportunities to see Gavaskar bestride the stage.

After all, he made almost twice as many appearances against England and played more often against the West Indies and, despite historic enmities and consequent programming hiatuses, neighbouring Pakistan.

Discounting his appearances for the barely-remembered Rest of the World team against Australia in 1971-72, Gavaskar played 32 Tests in six years and nine months before first confronting an Australian team in a traditional Test match

- at Brisbane in December 1977. And he had played 60 Tests and scored 20 of his 34 centuries in eight years and six months before he first played a home Test against Australia at Madras in September 1979.

It is hardly surprising, therefore, that there are those within the Australian cricket cricket community who feel they were cheated by the actions of a succession of Australian administrators thinly disguised as Anglophiles and ignorant of cricket in Asia and the emergence of a new world order within the game.

And while such misguidedness has been addressed if not yet redressed by the more recent governors of Australian cricket - following Gavaskar's retirement, regrettably - the bonds between Australia and India are not as strong as history suggests they should be and Australia's visit to India in 1998 will be their first for Test matches in 12 years.

Aside from the cognoscenti, few are aware of the significant role played by Australians in the formative years of Indian cricket. At the behest of the Maharaja of Patiala, Victorian all-rounder Frank Tarrant organised the first Australian team to tour India in 1935-36 and, furthermore, was consulted on all matters from the highly specialised coaching of India's first Test team to the preparation of turf pitches and umpiring. Indeed, Tarrant umpired India's first home Test match (against England) at Bombay in 1933-34. And Leo O'Brien, at the age of 88 Australia's oldest living Test cricketer in 1995, was the first cricket coach at India's National Institute of Sports at Patiala in 1961 and 1962.

Like so many cricketers of his generation Gavaskar was reared on the phenomenal achievements of Sir Donald Bradman and this despite the fact the semi-divine only once stepped onto Indian soil - at Calcutta's Dum Dum Airport in 1953 on his way to England to cover the Ashes series for the London Daily Mail. (Gavaskar was born four months after Bradman played his last first-class match at Adelaide in March 1949).

So while Gavaskar needed to bide his time the fates decreed that not only would he prosper against Australia but he would become acquainted with Sir Donald and, in the end, eclipse the great man's record of 29 centuries in Test cricket.

To some extent, Australia's perception of Gavaskar has been influenced by Sir Donald's high opinion of the Indian maestro. Such is Sir Donald's stature that he has long had the last word on all ideologies, issues and identities within the game and he was captivated by Gavaskar from the time of their first meeting at Adelaide in 1971. Indeed, Gavaskar has never forgotten Sir Donald's welcoming and reassuring wink and riposte to Gary Sobers who had teasingly referred to the need for the "little blokes" to stick together. "These big blokes have the power but we little ones have the footwork, huh?" observed Bradman (standing 5 ft. $6^3/_4$ ins.) to Gavaskar (5 ft. $4^3/_4$ ins). So were sown the seeds of friendship which crossed continents and cultures as well as the years and in 1986 Sir Donald derived great pleasure in presenting to Gavaskar a silver salver to commemorate his scoring the 100th Test century at Adelaide Oval. In his tribute Sir Donald said: "Not only has he (Gavaskar) delighted us with his skill and technique but he has also delighted us with his sportsmanship." Fourteen years earlier Sir Donald had presented the 22-year-old Gavaskar with a trophy for being the most accomplished fieldsman in the Rest of the World team and, furthermore, had happily advised him on important matters of technique.

With the exception of an unproductive and rather fraught visit to Australia in 1980-81 Gavaskar maintained a heady standard of excellence throughout his campaigns with Australia. He scored a century in his first Indo-Australian Test at Brisbane in December 1977 and averaged 50 or more in his four other series including a Bradmanesque 117.33 in 1985-86 when he unleashed an unconquered 166 before Sir Donald at Adelaide Oval.

If 1985-86 was a particularly memorable season for Gavaskar, the summer of 1980-81, the only time in his 47-Test career as captain he led in Australia, was utterly forgettable. Not only did he lose the aura of invincibility by averaging 19.66 from six hands in three Tests, but he was embroiled in an umpiring controversy which was headlined around the world and briefly caused some critics to question his sportsmanship. So incensed was he at a leg before wicket decision given against him that he persuaded his opening partner Chetan Chauhan to leave the field with him on the fourth day of the third Test match at Melbourne. Had it not been for the decisive intervention of the team management India may have forfeited the Test match. In the end, they won by 59 runs and so levelled the series to provide some balm for a wounded and contrite Gavaskar.

Always sensitive to the mocking of sub-continental umpires and a longtime and strident advocate of an international panel Gavaskar was again critical of Australian umpires during 1991-92 when working as an insightful and sometimes provocative television commentator and newspaper columnist.

Australians did not admire Gavaskar only for his candour, strong sense of team and awesome run-gathering but for his technical competence and brilliance and precise and pragmatic professionalism so redolent of Sir Donald.

Indeed, they have a colourful history of supporting the loyal and self-effacing "little battler" against his adversaries and they thrilled to the fact that Gavaskar confronted the fastest and most intimidating of bowlers without the protection of a helmet.

They had the utmost respect for his physical courage and indeed, for his moral courage so often demonstrated by a robust defence (and promotion) of sub-continental cricket which be believed too often was treated with a shameful indifference by the game's Anglo-centric and elitist establishment. In a contributed article in 1990 he wrote: "An open mind will respect our enormous love for the game and its players and will appreciate the level of discomfort spectators will endure just to be able to see a game of cricket. Visiting cricketers blessed with open minds will be rewarded with an adulation far beyond their wildest dreams. ...The unfortunate part of the developed world is the undeveloped mind, not willing to learn and soak in new experiences."

Gavaskar's unselfconscious patriotism and, for all the privileges of his life in Bombay, apparent belief in egalitarianism also appealed to the earthiest of Australians who could scarcely conceal their delight when, in the first instance, he loudly refused his honorary life membership of the Marylebone Cricket Club after being treated with disdain by one the infamous Lord's gatemen.

Gavaskar, the cricketer of the 890 million people of India, further endeared himself to Australians by so vigorously embracing Allan Border, the cricketer of 18 million people Down Under. He was always profuse in his praise of the little left-hander (Border stands at 5 ft. 9 ins.) who was destined to eclipse his aggregate record of runs and in January 1994 especially travelled to Sydney to give the keynote address at a lavish tribute dinner to Border.

At the time Gavaskar said: "He (Border) is a cricketer after my own heart and has shown right through his career what a good cricketer should be."

As it happened Border had been appointed to the Board of the Australia-India Council which was set up by the Australian Government in 1992 to encourage and support contacts between Australia and India and to increase levels of knowledge and understanding between the peoples of the two countries. To this end and quite characteristically, Gavaskar answered a call to manage an Indian invitation teams in a series of matches against Australia's finest young players in 1994.

At a time when so many of the traditional values and virtues of the glorious and ancient game were being undermined it was reassuring to realise two of its contemporary deities were good mates.

And, in the Australian idiom, bloody good blokes with it.

With a Caribbean Eye: The Little Master   MICHAEL GIBBES

It is now more than 24 years ago since I first witnessed Sunil Manohar Gavaskar in action on the cricket field. I was privileged to be among the large crowd on that memorable day at the Queen's Park Oval (March 6, 1971) when the diminutive opening batsman made his debut against Gary Sobers' West Indies team in the second Test of that series - and he was 21 years 208 days old at the time and the cynosure of all eyes.

Gavaskar's reputation as a promising and gifted opener had preceded him even before his arrival in the Caribbean with Ajit Wadekar's side that year, the third Indian touring team to visit the region. There was keen disappointment when a finger infection forced him to miss the opening Test of the series at Sabina Park, Jamaica - a match which was drawn after the home team had surprisingly followed on.

In his Test debut at the Queen's Park Oval - he took the place of reserve opener Kenia Jayantilal - Gavaskar played two impressive cameo innings of 65 (one of off-spinner Jack Noreiga's nine victims) and then 67 not out, a display which steered India safely home to a seven-wicket victory. This memorable triumph marked the very first occasion on which his country had defeated the West Indies in a Test match. Since the inaugural series between the two countries on the sub-continent in 1948-49, the Windies had won no less than 12 of the previous 24 clashes, with the remainder left drawn - and Gavaskar was one of the architects of a victory which boosted India's self-image. A century by Dilip Sardesai and excellent bowling by the spin trio Bedi, Prasanna and Venkataraghavan contributed, along with Gavaskar's showing, to seal the West Indies' fate.

Few West Indians who saw this Test could have been left in any doubt that a new star was emerging on cricket's horizon, one who seemed destined - given good health and freedom from niggling injuries - to become the lynchpin, the avatar, of his country's cricket fortunes. It was unmistakably clear to me that his burgeoning talent would carve out a proud place for him in the cricket sun in the years that lay ahead. So assured was his strokeplay, so sound his technique against the new ball propelled by Vanburn Holder, Grayson Shillingford and Sobers himself. And he was equally assured when facing the spin attack of Noreiga and Arthur Barrett. One recalls as though it were yesterday, Gavaskar's composure, his confident demeanour and his admirable approach to his new role on the international stage.

All of this may sound to some as mere hindsight, an overview sanctioned by his future prolific achievements during a career which spanned some 17 years - but human memory, fallible as it sometimes can be, is not playing tricks here. He early showed a batting style, panache and intense powers of concentration which marked him out as exceptional, as no run-of-the-mill opening batsman. At all events, his role in that historic win in Port-of-Spain on March 10, 1971 had been a significant one, a fact not lost on the game's cognoscenti in the Caribbean nor indeed the amateur armchair critics.

Gavaskar, by virtue of his batting skill, personality, physical courage and ability to entertain cricket crowds, quickly became one of the most popular players ever to visit the Caribbean - and no more so than at the Queen's Park Oval and Bourda, two Test venues where there is a large element of spectators of East Indian extraction. He became a hero overnight to all ethnic groups, let it be stressed, but to none more so than those who happened to share his culture and historical origins. Though the crowds naturally wanted to see the home team win, they warmed to the class and batting prowess of the dapper Gavaskar who, after his baptism of fire, went from strength to strength and enjoyed a phenomenal tour both in the statistical sense and as an emerging folk-hero.

And here we may observe that in a special context, the subtle demands of culture can often (perhaps unconsciously) outweigh and transcend the demands of nationality and geographical loyalties. To those narrow-minded critics who bemoaned the spectacle of local Indians seeking to garland Gavaskar and shower him with gifts of money when he scored a century (as he was to often at the Queen's Park Oval!), let me simply ask them to answer a simple phenomenon which they conveniently tend to ignore: why do black West Indians living in England - not recent immigrants, but those who are actually English citizens by birth howl for English blood and cracked ribs when Holding thunders in to bowl to Boycott or Greig, or to update the scenario, when Ambrose roars in to bowl at Mike Atherton? The parallel is obvious: cultural ties often take priority over citizenship - and this trend may take centuries to be totally eradicated. The ideal to strive for is to applaud excellence on display by either team, eschewing churlish partisan loyalties which can sometimes lead to acrimony and petty-mindedness by self-confessed bigots.

For Sunil, that 1971 tour was a case of "roses, roses all the way," as he maintained his prolific form throughout the series (which incidentally India won 1-0). He was destined to visit the Caribbean as an active player on three occasions, returning with Bishen Bedi's team in 1976 and again in 1983 when India were led by Kapil Dev. Though Gavaskar went on to captain his country no fewer than 47 times, he was never at the helm in a Caribbean Test series. In 1989 he returned to the region with Dilip Vengsarkar's side, but on this occasion as a member of the media, with his playing days having ended two years earlier. I had the pleasure of meeting him in the Press Box during this tour - and he was gracious enough to thank me for a laudatory article I wrote about him in the "Trinidad Guardian". Gavaskar was back in Trinidad in 1995 on the occasion of Indian Arrival Day celebrations, an honoured guest in a land he himself considers his second home. It was a thrill to renew acquaintance with this charming man who may have his critics (who, pray, doesn't) but he has over the years been a tremendous asset to Indian cricket, and one of the game's immortals.

In the third Test of the 1971 series at Bourda, Georgetown,

he slammed 116 and 64 not out in a drawn game - and then in Barbados he registered his solitary failure in this tour, a victim of paceman Uton Dowe for 1. But in the second innings, the runs flowed once more, a sparkling 117 not out. Back to the Queen's Park Oval for the final Test, the Bombay opener covered himself with glory, achieving the rare feat of scoring a century in each innings: 124 and 220, his first "double ton" at this level. So Gavaskar had ended his annus mirablis, (his year of wonders) in spectacular style, amassing a mind-boggling aggregate of 774 runs at a phenomenal average of 154.80, and all this, mind you, in only four Test matches. Comparisons were being drawn in West Indian cricket circles of other prolific batsmen who had previously topped 700 runs in a Caribbean series: the great George Headley, 703 in 1930 (4 Tests); Everton Weekes, 716 in 1953 (5 Tests); Clyde Walcott, 827 in 1955 (5 Tests); Sobers, 824 in 1959 and 709 in 1960 - all Bradmanesque performances!

The truth is, Gavaskar had set such high standards of consistency in 1971 that he gravely disappointed his admirers on his visits to England both in 1971 and 1974 where the strange, unfamiliar nature of the variable pitches tested his technique and his relative inexperience. It was not until the latter part of the decade that the runs began to flow again. As was to become customary, (with one notable exception), Sunil thrived again on a diet of West Indian bowling on his second visit to the Caribbean in 1976. And once again, he made the Queen's Park Oval in Trinidad his "happy hunting ground", scoring a scintillating 156 in the second Test and 102 in the third, an innings which helped India score 406 on the final day to triumph by six wickets. Only Bradman's great 1948 team had done so before. Lloyd, it is true, declared his second innings prematurely, but India, spearheaded by disciplined batting from Gavaskar, Amarnath and Vishwanath, seized their chance to level the series. But in the deciding Test at Sabina, the atrocious abuse of bouncers by Holding led Bedi - worried about the physical safety of his batsmen- to close his second innings at 97 (with five batsmen absent hurt!). So the home team, in dubious style, won the series 2-1.

Gavaskar scored 66 and 2 at Sabina and totalled 390 runs at a commendable average of 55.71. His test aggregate at the Queen's Park Oval, including the 1983 visit when he suffered a loss of form, is a superb 661 runs (average 94.42).

His form deserted him on his return in 1983 when Kapil Dev led the team: nine knocks yielded a paltry 240 runs - and only at Bourda, where he made an undefeated 147, did he do himself justice. Was he peeved at being deprived of the captaincy, as some critics have suggested? The media made a fuss over his alleged rivalry with the younger Kapil Dev; but much of this was pure speculation. The real answer may simply be that he suffered a diminution in form which sometimes affects even the great ones. After all, as they say, even Homer nods on occasion. The torrid pace attack posed major problems but on the West Indies tour of India in 1983-84, Gavaskar recaptured his form with a vengeance. Earlier, against a team without the Packer stars in 1979, he once more demonstrated his predilection for Caribbean bowling, garnering 732 runs: including 205 and 73 at Bombay, 120 at Delhi and a century in each innings at Calcutta. And in 1983-84, his final outing against Lloyd's team, he totalled 505 runs, hitting his highest Test score of 236 not out in the final Test at the Chepauk Stadium, Madras.

It was an historic, though controversial innings, for in it he finally eclipsed Bradman's record of 29 Test hundreds. It was also Sunil's fourth double century, following on his feats at the Queen's Park Oval, Bombay and the Oval in London in 1979 where his brilliant 221 in an improbable victory charge almost carried India to an incredible victory against Botham, Willis, Hendrick and Edmonds. His panache on that occasion impressed even an unbelieving English press who were eloquent in their praise for his technique and dedication in the face of adversity.

Dedication, technical skill (revealed in a wide repertoire of strokes) and a professional approach have been the hallmarks of his batting, allied to admirable self-confidence against hostile bowling. These qualities must be kept in mind when analysing his valid claim to pre-eminence among contemporary opening batsmen.

But more than this, his superlative record achieved against an awesome battery of West Indian fast bowlers speaks volumes for his stature. Between 1971 and 1987 - when he quit international cricket at the age of 38 - the Little Master (a sobriquet which he acquired during his first tour of the Caribbean) crossed swords with pacemen of the calibre of Holding, Roberts, Garner, Marshall, Sylvester Clarke, Holder and Winston Davis, handling their menacing thunderbolts with assurance, if not with consummate ease and technical perfection and aplomb. He was too late on the scene to face Wes Hall and Charlie Griffith; too early to take on Ambrose, Walsh, Patterson and Ian Bishop. That he prospered against such an array of good fast bowlers is eloquent testimony to his indisputable class, technical proficiency and (not least) physical courage (with no benefit of a helmet and visor) for during his career, as Mike Coward aptly states, The West Indies in the Clive Lloyd era and beyond, were "the power brokers of the modern game".

Widening the scope of the argument to embrace other Test-playing nations, Gavaskar made 8 centuries versus Australia, with Lillee and Thomson, Hogg and Max Walker, while he also faced the pace of Imran Khan and Richard Hadlee.

Yet it is significant to observe that 13 of his 34 Test centuries were made against the West Indies and more than a quarter of his final tally of 10,122 runs which remained a world record until eclipsed recently by the durable Allan Border of Australia. In all first class matches, Sunil scored 25,834 runs with a top score of 340 - made at Bombay versus Bengal in the 1982 Ranji Trophy tournament. Both his Test match and first-class averages exceed 50. But one coveted target eluded him : he is not among that elite band of 23 batsmen listed in Wisden, who have made 100 centuries during their careers; he ended with 81 centuries, more than any of fellow countrymen - and his amazing consistency is shown by the fact that he hit 20 centuries in his first 50 Test matches, a feat that precious few players can match. Between 1975 and 1987, Gavaskar made 106 consecutive Test appearances and among Indian cricketers, only Kapil Dev (131) has exceeded his total of 125 matches.

Those achievements are clearly conclusive in confirming the Little Master as undeniably the greatest batsman to play Test cricket for India, still adulated and given VIP treatment by his admirers in his homeland - and indeed regarded as a folk hero. I emphasise "for India", since his two main rivals, Ranjitsinjhi and his nephew Duleepsinhji (both master-batsmen in the view of revered critics of the pre-war era) never represented India, the country of their birth, playing all their cricket on English fields for Cambridge University, Sussex and England. Other eminent Indian batsmen since those early days would include C.K.Nayudu, Vijay Merchant, Pataudi Snr., Umrigar and the precocious talented star of the 1990's, Sachin Tendulkar. But I have no hesitation in naming Gavaskar (born in Bombay on July 10, 1949) as Numero Uno among the greatest Test willow-wielders produced by India.

It is often quite misleading to judge a player's worth by relying only on statistics - by that yardstick, pedestrian batsmen like Barrington and Lawry can lord it over geniuses like Trumper and Wooley, to name but two giants. Statistics are in reality the bare bones of batsmanship, as R.C.Robertson-Glasgow has wisely pointed out; they often obscure the flesh and blood of genuine class and prevent us from seeing "the men without their arithmetic". But by the same token, Test figures are surely a reliable guide to greatness as in the case of Don Bradman, Hobbs, Hammond, Headley, Sobers and Gavaskar.

On three occasions, the Indian opener made centuries in each innings of a Test, a unique feat. And it may be many years before his total of 34 hundreds is surpassed, even with rampant superstars like Brian Lara and Sachin Tendulkar still in the morning of their careers, and with talent to burn. It won't be an easy record to eclipse, even with the plethora of Test matches in vogue these days!

The Gavaskar I recall watching did not try to dominate bowlers in the blood-and-thunder, belligerent way that old timers say Bradman did, and it was alien to his thinking to tear the new ball attack apart in the manner of say, a Greenidge or a Roy Marshall were wont to do. He was at times content to wage a war of attrition; to harvest his energies shrewdly on his way to a century; to eschew the cut stroke until well set at the crease, and to utilise his superb technique in seeing the pace attack off. An accomplished technician in the manner of Boycott, not a cavalier willow-wielder like Kanhai in his younger days. At times, of course, he would cut loose with a flurry of audacious strokes that took the breath away. But always adaptable, serene and competitive, a master of his craft.

Comparisons of him with Bradman (whom regrettably, I never saw in action) are perhaps inevitable, given their consistency and prolific achievements. But these two master-batsmen were clearly products of two totally different eras, and this essential fact was discernible in their style of play and tempo. Some critics who saw all three men at the wicket, see Gavaskar as a cross between Bradman and Geoff Boycott of Yorkshire and England fame, another supremely dedicated player who lacked the Indian opener's natural ability but more than compensated for this with his astounding commitment to perfection of his technique.

Yet, however much one admires Gavaskar's skill, it is only fair to remember that while he took 94 Test matches to reach his target of the Don's 29 centuries, the incomparable Bradman scored his tally of 29 in only 51 matches. The disparity in their final averages is also revealing: Bradman 99.94 in a mere 52 Tests; Gavaskar 51.12 in 125 matches. The Australian slammed 12 double centuries (including two triples versus

England), while the Bombay star scored four. Both were short, little men in physical stature; Gavaskar a mere 5 ft. 4.75 ins (164 cm) in height.

The Little master was a model for all budding young batsmen to emulate. He put a bloom on the orthodox with a cast iron defence against the new ball and was also excellent in playing the spinners, nimble in footwork and with immense powers of concentration. He could cut, cover drive or pull with the best of them, but normally eschewed the risky hook stroke. Only injury kept him out of an Indian Test team during his halcyon days - and he was as indispensable to India's strategy as Boycott was to England's or Viv Richards to the conquering West Indies side during the years of Caribbean plenty.

Among the opening batsmen I have seen in the period of my attendance at Test matches (1948-1995), the only players who loom as Sunil's rivals for sheer perfection of technique are Len Hutton, Boycott, Hunte, David Boon and Cowdrey. The graceful Jeff Stollmeyer and Rae, Greenidge and Haynes were formidable and successful as pairs - but I regret never seeing Barry Richards in action, to say nothing of pre-war titans like Hobbs and Sutcliffe or Challenor.

After his playing days were over, Gavaskar exchanged the willow for the pen, so maintaining close touch with the game he loved. As a media man, his syndicated column is at times filled with shrewd comment; at other times vitriolic and controversial. But he was always determined to speak his mind, candid and sincere - and his dry wit and sound analysis of the modern game are added assets. He is the author of four entertaining cricket books.

Let the Trinidadian calypsonian, Lord Relator have the last word about a cricketer who stole away West Indian hearts in 1971 when he burst upon the cricket world in dramatic fashion, announcing his arrival with impeccable credentials and a harvest of runs in what was for him a memorable season, scoring 774 runs and frustrating Sobers' beleaguered bowlers:

> *It was Gavaskar, the real master,*
> *Just like a wall,*
> *We couldn't out Gavaskar at all.*

Poetic licence, of course, since he was dismissed on five occasions - but at what a price to Caribbean hopes of saving the series! Sunil Gavaskar is a man to admire - and his place in cricket history is irrevocably secure, the highest gem in the crown of Indian cricket and an adornment to the Commonwealth game. The West Indies public have a special place reserved in their hearts for this great opening batsman who proved a fine ambassador for his country.

Statistical Appendix Gavaskar's Career Record

GAVASKAR'S TEST CENTURIES : 34

	Test No.	Runs	Versus	Venue	Series
1	2	116	WI	George Town	70-71
2	3	117*	WI	Bridge Town	70-71
3	4	124	WI	Port of Spain	70-71
4	4	220	WI	Port of Spain	70-71
5	13	101	Eng	Manchester	74
6	18	116	NZ	Auckland	75-76
7	22	156	WI	Port of Spain	75-76
8	23	102	WI	Port of Spain	75-76
9	25	119	NZ	Bombay	76-77
10	32	108	Eng	Bombay	76-77
11	33	113	Aust	Brisbane	77-78
12	34	127	Aust	Perth	77-78
13	35	118	Aust	Melbourne	77-78
14	40	111	Pak	Karachi	78-79
15	40	137	Pak	Karachi	78-79
16	41	205	WI	Bombay	78-79
17	43	107	WI	Calcutta	78-79
18	43	182*	WI	Calcutta	78-79
19	45	120	WI	Delhi	78-79
20	50	221	Eng	The Oval	79
21	54	115	Aust	Delhi	79-80
22	56	123	Aust	Bombay	79-80
23	61	166	Pak	Madras	79-80
24	71	172	Eng	Bangalore	81-82
25	79	155	S.Lanka	Madras	81-82
26	82	127*	Pak	Faisalabad	82-83
27	88	147*	WI	Georgetown	82-83
28	91	103*	Pak	Bangalore	83-84
29	95	121	WI	Delhi	83-84
30	99	236*	WI	Madras	83-84
31	110	166*	Aust	Adelaide	85-86
32	112	172	Aust	Sydney	85-86
33	118	103	Aust	Bombay	86-87
34	119	176	S.Lanka	Kanpur	86-87

TEST MATCH PERFORMANCE - Series by Series Record

Year	India Vs	Test	Innings	N.O.	Total Runs	H.S	Century	Half Century	Average
1970-71	West Indies	4	8	3	774	220	4	3	154.80
1971	England	3	6	0	144	57	-	2	24.00
1972-73	England	5	10	1	224	69	-	2	24.88
1974	England	3	6	0	217	101	1	1	36.16
1974-75	West Indies	2	4	0	108	86	-	1	27.00
1975-76	New Zealand	3	5	1	266	116	1	1	66.50
1975-76	West Indies	4	7	0	390	156	2	1	55.71
1976-77	New Zealand	3	6	0	259	119	1	1	43.16
1976-77	England	5	10	0	394	108	1	2	39.40
1977-78	Australia	5	9	0	450	127	3	-	50.00
1978-79	Pakistan	3	6	1	447	137	2	2	89.40
1978-79	West Indies	6	9	1	732	205	4	1	91.53
1979	England	4	7	0	542	221	1	4	77.43
1979-80	Australia	6	8	0	425	123	2	2	53.12
1979-80	Pakistan	6	11	1	529	166	1	2	52.90
1979-80	England	1	2	0	73	49	-	-	36.50
1980-81	Australia	3	6	0	118	70	-	1	19.66
1980-81	New Zealand	3	5	0	126	53	-	1	25.20
1981-82	England	6	9	1	500	172	1	3	62.50
1982	England	3	3	0	74	48	-	-	24.66
1982-83	Sri Lanka	1	2	1	159	155	1	-	159.00
1982-83	Pakistan	6	10	1	434	127	1	3	48.22
1982-83	West Indies	5	9	1	240	147	1	-	30.00
1983-84	Pakistan	3	5	1	264	103	1	2	66.00
1983-84	West Indies	6	11	1	505	236	2	1	50.50
1984-85	Pakistan	2	3	0	120	48	-	-	40.00
1984-85	England	5	8	0	140	65	-	1	17.50
1985-86	Sri Lanka	3	6	1	186	52	-	1	37.20
1985-86	Australia	3	4	1	352	172	2	-	117.33
1986	England	3	6	0	175	54	-	1	29.16
1986-87	Australia	3	4	0	205	103	1	1	51.25
1986-87	Sri Lanka	3	3	0	255	176	1	1	85.00
1986-87	Pakistan	4	6	0	295	96	-	3	49.16
TOTAL		125	214	16	10122	236	34	45	51.12

OVERALL RECORD VS EACH COUNTRY

Opponents	Test	Innings	N.O.	Total Runs	H.S	Average	Century	Half Century	Ct.
vs. Pakistan	24	41	4	2089	166	56.45	5	12	19
vs. New Zealand	9	16	1	651	119	43.40	2	3	11
vs. Sri Lanka	7	11	2	600	178	66.66	2	3	7
vs. West Indies	27	48	6	2749	236*	65.45	13	7	17
vs. England	38	67	2	2483	221	38.20	4	18	35
vs. Australia	20	31	1	1550	172	51.66	8	4	19
	125	214	16	10122	236*	51.12`	34	45	108

HOME AND AWAY RECORD

	Test	Innings	N.O.	Total Runs	H.S	Average	Century	Half Century
Home	65	108	7	5067	236*	50.6	16	23
Away	60	106	9	5055	221	52.11	18	22
	125	214	16	10122	236*	51.12	34	45

MILESTONES

Runs	Tests	Innings	Opponent	Venue	Series
1,000	11	21	Eng	Kanpur	1972-73
2,000	23	44	WI	Port of Spain	1975-76
3,000	34	66	Aust	Perth	1977-78
4,000	43	81	WI	Calcutta	1987-79
5,000	52	95	Aust	Bangalore	1979-80
6,000	65	117	Aust	Adelaide	1980-81
7,000	80	140	Pak	Lahore	1982-83
8,000	95	166	WI	Delhi	1983-84
9,000	110	192	Aust	Adelaide	1985-86
10,000	124	212	Pak	Ahmedabad	1986-87

RANJI TROPHY RECORD

Season	I	N.O.	Runs	H.S.	Average	C
1969-70	3	1	141	114	70.50	1
1970-71	3	-	307	176	102.33	2
1971-72	5	-	494	282	98.80	2
1972-73	12	2	579	160	57.90	3
1973-74	9	0	248	84	27.55	-
1974-75	6	1	203	96*	40.60	-
1975-76	5	1	510	190	127.50	3
1976-77	9	1	398	120	49.75	1
1978-79	6	-	377	204	62.83	2
1979-80	11	1	491	153	49.10	1
1981-82	8	1	632	340	90.29	2
1983-84	9	3	541	206*	108.20	2
1984-85	7	3	399	106	99.75	1
1985-86	1	-	15	15	15.00	-
TOTAL	94	14	5335	340	66.68	20

TEST RECORD AS CAPTAIN

Opponents	Season	Matches	Lost	Won	Drawn
New Zealand	1976-77	1	0	1	0
West Indies	1978-79	6	0	1	5
Australia	1979-80	6	0	2	4
Pakistan	1979-80	5	0	2	3
Australia	1980-81	3	1	1	1
New Zealand	1980-81	3	1	0	2
England	1981-82	6	0	1	5
England	1982	3	1	0	2
Sri Lanka	1982-83	1	0	0	1
Pakistan	1982-83	6	3	0	3
Pakistan	1984-85	2	0	0	2
England	1984-85	5	2	1	2
TOTAL		47	8	9	30

Sources of Reference

Bhogle, H: *Azhar*, Penguin Books India 1994

Blunden, E: *Cricket Country*, Pavilion Books 1985

Bose, M: *A History of Indian Cricket*, Andre Deutsch 1990

Brearley, M: *The Art of Captaincy*, Hodder & Stoughton Ltd. 1985

Bright-Holmes, J (ed): *The Joy of Cricket*, Secker and Warburg 1984

Clark, C.D: *The Record-breaking Gavaskar*, David and Charles Inc. U.S.A.

Dev, Kapil: *The World of Kapil Dev*, UBSP Distributors Ltd. 1992

Doshi, Dilip: *Spin Punch*, Rupa 1991

Frindall, Bill (ed): *The Wisden Book of Test Cricket -*
(2 volumes), Queen Ann Press Book

Gavaskar, S.M: *Sunny Days*, Rupa 1976
                 Idols, Rupa 1983
                 Runs 'n Ruins, Rupa 1984
                 One Day Wonders, Rupa 1986

Greig, Tony: *Test Match Cricket, A Personal View*, The Hamlyn Publishing Group Ltd. 1977

Grimshaw, Anna (ed): *C.L.R. James Cricke*t, W.H. Allen & Co. 1986

Heller, Erich: *The Disinherited Mind*, Penguin Books 1961

Holding, M and Cozier, T: *Wispering Death*, West Indies Publishers 1993

James, C.L.R: *Beyond a Boundary*, Hutchinson 1963

Keynes, S and Lapidge, M: (translated and introduced by) *Alfred The Great*, Penguin Books 1983

Lemmon, D: *The Guinness Book of Test Cricket Captains*, Guinness Publishing

Manley, Michael: *The History of West Indian Cricket*, West Indies Publishing

Moraes, Dom: *Sunil Gavaskar - An Illustrated Biography*, MacMillan India 1987

Singh, Vickram: *Test Cricket, End of The Road*

Sivaramakrishnan, S: *Sunil Gavaskar, His Life, Career and Contributions to Cricket* (doctoral dissertation, Alagappa University College of Physical Education 1989)

Tenant, Ivo: *Imran Khan*, H.F. and G. Witherby 1994

Wadhmaney, K.R: *Test Cricketers of India*, Siddarth Publications 1995

Wilde, Simon: *Ranji, A Genius Rich and Strange*

Wilde, Simon: *Letting Rip, The Fast-Bowling Threat from Lillee to Waqar*, H.F and G. Witherby 1994

Annuals:
> *Wisden Cricketers' Almanac*
> *Benson and Hedges Cricket Year*

Magazines / Periodicals:
> *The Cricketer*
> *Sportsweek*
> *Sportstar*
> *Sportsworld*
> *India Today*
> *Wisden Cricket Monthly*

News:
> *Times of India*
> *Hindu*
> *Midday*
> *Indian Express*
> *Telegraph (Calcutta)*

Index